Daily Doses of Deborah Volume III

31 days of daily devotions, meditations, recipes, tricks, thoughts and ideas from deborahmillspsychic

Deborah A. Mills, PhD

Over the years, I write a daily blog, daily email out. My intention, my hope is that in the early morning, we start our day with positive thoughts, ideas, hopes, dreams for the brand new day. Here in Volume 3, we continue to seek to send the message of hope, faith, dreams, possibilities, magick in our lives. As with all deborahmillspsychic products, the book has been charged in the moonlight, kissed by Venus to bring the magick in our lives. Love ya, Me!

Written by Deborah Mills, PhD

Editor, Sharon Cook
Published March, 2014

DAY 1:

"A little behind, I'm a little late, I've made others, myself to wait. Lives busy busy, like a New York, LA city, the wait helps to slow down. Slow down the pace, find the right path to race, as balance, hope is the way to faith."
~ deborahmills 2014 Poems for lessons of hope

"Life was always a matter of waiting for the right moment to act." ~ Paulo Coelho

"Perhaps all the dragons of our lives are princesses who are only waiting to see us once beautiful and brave." ~ Rainer Maria Rilke

Long before the Reformers, the Zealots came; the dragons roamed the Mother Earth free and clear. Fearsome, many people saw the dragons as something to be afraid of because truly these entities were bigger than life, fire breathing, fierce to see, ferocious to hear roar. In truth, each kingdom had a dragon of the land's own, to protect at the caves before the gates, so enemies cannot reach the town. Yet as time went on, people became afraid of the very entity the gods had given to protect them, decided to destroy the dragons. The gods were very worried about this so the powers shrunk the dragons to dragonflies. Still when troubles come, brother dragonfly can come. Our lives are like this at times. We have changes, or we wait, seeing thls as a dragon, to hurt us. The problems, the dragons come to cause us intense pain, to destroy what we so long to receive in our lives. Yet, often times, the wait has become as dragon fly , sent only at odd times, to give us time to recoup, to find the right path, to slow down a minute, so we are so sure not to make any mistakes. AND the most important, we wait so he/she won't continue to make mistakes. The wait doesn't mean we don't receive the dream, just so the Great Spirit can bring about the very, absolute best. If we, as people, can step back, see the dragon as a 3rd party observer, for what is the greater good, we will be thankful for the wait, not hurt in heartache, but anxious, longing to see what great good changes will come through the dragon's fire.

Animal totem of the Day: Komodo Dragon.

One of the few dragons left to us without being totally shrunk, Sister Komodo still can look pretty fierce. She looks as a dinosaur, reminding us that the past does matter, is not totally wiped out, but also that this wait will pass. Being the only "real" dragon to still exist, she reminds us we will survive, will move forward. Quick decisions can be made after the waiting time, with her medicine. She reminds us that changes can be good, but the love, or the hope can still linger, the good parts of our past can remain. Her medicine is quiet, gentle, not overly aggressive, reminding us that words carry power. We can hurt more than a punch or a bite with our harsh, quick words.

Stone of the Day: Agate.
1. Blue lace, 2. Black, 3. Green, 4. Fire moss - this is a grounding stone to center, to balance. Blue will help with truth and clarity. This is also a hard stone of Protection. Zodiac: Gemini, Virgo. Planet: Moon. Element: Earth. Chakra: Crown Chakra. Planet: Pluto. Element: Air, Fire. Origin: Botswana.

Herb of the Day: Alfalfa.
Alfalfa (Medicavo Sativa) Gender: Feminine. Planet: Venus. Element: Earth. Prosperity, Anti-hunger, Money. Brings in money and protects against financial misfortune. Harvest a small quantity at the full moon. Dry and burn in the cauldron. Place ashes in a magickal amulet. This plant is rich in vitamins such as A, C, B1, B6 E and K as well as proteins, calcium, carotene, zinc, iron and potassium. It acts as a diuretic and a digestive as it is slightly laxative in nature. Helps with heart issues, and is a natural help for high blood pressure.

Recipe of the day: *"Grapefruit and Avocado Shrimp Salad"*
Ingredients:
2 pink grapefruits: peeled and sectioned
1 large ripe avocado: Peeled, diced, pitted
1 cup alfalfa sprouts
1 lemon, juiced
3 Tablespoons virgin olive oil
1 Ahi tuna: grilled, sliced thin
1 pinch salt, 1 pinch pepper
6 plump boiled jumbo shrimp
Directions:
1. Arrange 1/4 of the grapefruit sections and 1/4 of the diced avocado decoratively on a salad plate. Add tuna strips. Top with 1/4 cup of sprouts. Repeat with remaining grapefruit sections, avocado, and sprouts to make 4 salads.

2. Mix lemon juice, olive oil, salt, and black pepper in a small bowl; drizzle dressing over each salad.
3. Place around salad 6 plump boiled or grilled jumbo shrimp. Quick, fast, a good recipe as the Prep time is only 15 minutes, the cook time 15 minutes. Dinner is ready in 30 minutes. Healthy, low cal. What a treat.

*I found this recipe a long time ago, on **allsrecipe.com**, original created by Lisawas, I added a couple of twists and turns to it. So good.*

DAY 2:

"Inside my empty bottle I was constructing a lighthouse while all the others were making ships." ~ Charles Simic

"The world is round and the place which may seem like the end may also be only the beginning." ~ Ivy Baker Priest

"Won't you come into the garden? I would like my roses to see you." ~ Richard Brinsley Sheridan

Welcome to my morning, welcome to my world. Welcome to this new day where there are great possibilities of great, marvelous events, ideas, thoughts promises to be made, to be had, to be received. Oh yes, perhaps we have to dream dreams, hold our thoughts in our heart, giving complete total blind faith to the universe believing without a doubt that all things do work for the good, that higher power, spirit holds our best interests at heart, that there is something more out there that will guide us, help us. Oh yes, perhaps we do have to put trust in something, in others, that everyone isn't out to hurt us, to lie to us, to mislead us, but to try with all heart to give truly because this is the dreams given. Welcome to my love, my heart for this day is full of joy, open to any happiness we can find. We, as people, have a tendency to see the negative in so much. We have each one had hurts, deep rooted pains, problems, heartaches so deep, so long held that we are always waiting for the other shoe to drop, for something negative to happen yet again. Yet when the dark tries to creep over us, we can construct a lighthouse inside our mind. Instead of trying to make the ship to cause us to sail away from our problems, some say just give up, walk away, or worse some think of just leaving the mother Earth's plane altogether. Come into my world, where the problem is just another cross word puzzle, another jigsaw puzzle, another clue in the Life's game of Clue, to figure out the answer, to show us how this change will bring good things. Time oh yes, time we wait, but good things come to those who wait! So my loves, my friends, my hearts, welcome to my world, my garden, my roses are waiting to meet you.

Animal totem of the Day: Spider.

Sister Spider. We all know her well, there are times when some of us are afraid of her, but when she appears, we must realize she is all about balance. She is gentleness, as spider is very quiet, balanced with complete strength. Walking into a web she has woven, we often find it hard to break. Her totem is total creativeness as webs are intricate, lacey, beautiful, but the balance is practical, creating her home safe, provided for, reminds us that the past will help shape the future. Her medicine teaches us that we are infinite weaving our lives throughout time. This medicine reminds us to know that there is a plan to create our lives.

Stone of the Day: Amber.
Amber is not strictly a gemstone, but fossilized tree resin. Chakras: Sacral Chakra, Solar Plexus Chakra, Throat Chakra. Zodiac: Leo, Aquarius. Planet: Sun. Element: Fire. Gender: Male. Deities: Ra, Athena. Properties: Spiritual healing, protection, creative juices to flow.

Herb of the Day: Almond (Prunus dulcis).
Gender: Masculine. Planet: Mercury. Element: Air. Deities: Attis, Mercury, Thoth, Hermes. Magickal: Money, Prosperity, Wisdom. Almond wood makes excellent wands, ritual candlesticks, challis cups, altar board, especially for use in love magick. The Wiccans use this herb for hand-fastings or other rituals of union and/or marriage. Many herbalists recommend for overcoming alcohol dependency. I have heard that by eating almonds before a drinking spree, the alcohol doesn't affect as badly. Almonds, leaves, and wood may be used in money magick. Placing almonds in your pocket will lead you to treasures. Medicinal uses: Being a good source of vegetable protein and calcium usefulness in strengthening bones due to richness in bone-building mineral (Ca). Alpha-tocopherol, a component of vitamin E, present in almond is considered beneficial in prevention of cancer. Eating raw almonds or almond butter is a good source of protein which helps in anti-aging with the healing of memory loss, dementia.

Recipe of the Day: *"Heart – Antioxidant Almond Snack Mix"*
<u>Ingredients:</u>
3 cups multi grain cereal, such as Chex brand
3 cups multi grain fiber cereal twigs, such as fiber one
1 cup sweetened dried cranberries
¾ cup sweetened dark chocolate morsels
¾ cups almond butter

½ cups margarine (possible to use Smart spread)
¾ cup almond flour – (this can be bought at Kroger's, Frye's in the organic section)
¼ cup sliced almonds
¾ cups confectioner's sugar

Directions:

1. Line a large sheet pan with waxed paper. Place cereal and dried cranberries in a large re-sealable plastic bag. In a microwavable bowl, add chocolate chips, almond butter and enriched margarine spread (or butter). Microwave on High heat, uncovered, for 1 minute. Stir. Microwave for another 30 seconds; remove and stir until smooth.
2. Pour chocolate mixture into plastic bag, seal and shake to coat evenly. Add almond flour, sliced almonds and confectioner's sugar. Reseal and shake to coat. Spread mixture on waxed paper and cool completely. Refrigerate in an airtight container; mix can be stored for up to 1 week.

Fast, easy - pour in the bowl, then party hardy. Prep time: 10 minutes. Cook time: 1 minute.

I originally found this recipe put out by the Almond board of California. Who better do get good ideas from?

DAY 3:

"Firelight will not let you read fine stories but it's warm and you won't see the dust on the floor." ~ Irish Proverb

"We are each gifted in a unique and important way. It is our privilege and our adventure to discover our own special light." ~ Evelyn Dunbar

"Let there be light." ~ Genesis 1:3

Some say that we practice the ways of the old craft, of the old wise women from long ago. This may be true, but recently more people are turning back to the ways of organic, natural, products rather than the chemical based ones so perhaps we are in the way of the "new and improved" old ways. Yet most of us would prefer not to go back to no electricity, fire for heat, no way to reach our loved ones to find out if each one is okay. Yes, we don't cherish or relish the idea of going back to a time we would consider darkness. Yet yesterday we were hit with an ice storm. I used my technology as long as I could until the juice ran out, keeping on my iPhone charged as much as possible in case the nursing home should have to call me about my mother. After 5 pm the dogs and I were in complete darkness. Now, thank goodness I make candles so I had a full shelf stocked, I have a greenhouse so I had ceramic flower pots. So using tea lights, and 2 ceramic flower pots I built a heater. We were warm and well lit. Yet as I realized we might be in darkness, we had inner light. I had time to rest, much needed, meditate, and find inner light. See, I needed that rest; I needed that dark to heal toward the light. So when we find ourselves in darkness of any kind, problems we can see that this darkness gives us time to stop, meditate, find our answers, and then move toward the light.

Animal totem of the Day: Seal.

Bro seal is much like Bro buffalo. Natives use every part even the bladder as water bladder. Seal also tells us through his medicine to balance light and dark, playful, and work. His totem always reminds us to rest as they love to nap in the sun on a rock in the light.

Stone of the Day: Amethyst.
Amethyst is a variety of Quartz and is a 6th Anniversary gemstone. Chakras: Third Eye Chakra, Crown Chakra. Birthstone: February. Zodiac: Virgo, Sagittarius, Capricorn, Aquarius, Pisces. Planet: Jupiter. Element: Air, Water. Gender: Male. Deities: Mars, Jupiter, Mercury. Properties: calmness, quietness of spirit, gentle dreams and sleep, relieves anxiety.

Herb of the Day: Anise Seed.
Medicinal uses: Colds, congestion, cramps, lice, antibacterial, anti-cancer, aphrodisiac. Planet: Mercury/Jupiter. Element: Air. Deities: Apollo and Mercury. Gender: Male. Chakra: Throat, solar plexus. The magickal uses / properties are for contacting the Other Side, divination, love, passion, happiness.

Recipe of the Day: *"Crisp Anise Seed Butter Cookies"*
Ingredients:
4 cups all-purpose flour
1 tablespoon baking powder
1/8 teaspoon salt
1 cup butter softened (real butter rather than margarine is best)
1 cup white sugar
2 eggs
1 teaspoon vanilla extract (use real extract not imitation)
3 tablespoons anise seed – (use real anise seeds)
¼ cup white sugar (for decoration purposes)
1 teaspoon ground cinnamon (for decoration purposes)
Directions:
1. Sift together the flour, baking powder and salt; set aside. In a large bowl, cream together the butter and 1 cup sugar until smooth. Beat in the eggs one at a time then stir in the vanilla. Gradually mix in the sifted ingredients and anise seeds until well blended. Cover and chill for several hours or overnight.
2. Preheat the oven to 400 degrees F (200 degrees C). Grease cookie sheets. On a lightly floured surface, roll the dough out to 1/4 inch in thickness. Cut into desired shapes with cookie cutters. Place cookies 1- 1/2 inches apart onto cookie sheets. Sprinkle the tops with a mixture of the remaining 1/4 cup of sugar and cinnamon.
3. Bake for 8 to 10 minutes in the preheated oven, until light brown. Cool on baking sheets for a few minutes before removing to wire racks to cool completely.

The prep time for these are 20 minutes, cooking time is 8 minutes; they are ready in 1 hour.   Makes 50 cookies.

I discovered this recipe on ***allsrecipe.com****. Barbara Carrigan first printed this recipe. We added a few variations here and there when we make them for Grammee's Goodies to Go.*

DAY 4:

"There's a world where I can go And tell my secrets to In my room In my room In this world I lock out All my worries and my fears In my room In my room Do my dreaming and my scheming lie awake and pray Do my crying and my sighing laugh at yesterday Now it's dark and I'm alone But I won't be afraid In my room In my room" ~ Songwriters MARTIN, ERIC WILLIAM / USHER, GARY L. / WILSON, BRIAN / GAYLE, MICHELLE PATRICIA

Inside each of us is heartaches, pains, desires, hopes, fears, love. Our insides get tied up in turmoil, in knots as clearly as the knots in a rope tied to keep something bound up. Yet, we have also in ourselves the ability to find a place within, that we can go to, as well as make a place of sanctuary to find a place of comfort in our outer environment. Perhaps it is a place of worship. Perhaps it is a place in our home, down by the river, the lake, or up to the top of the mountains. Even if we can't physically go there right at the moment when we need to find peace, we can sit in quiet repose, clear our heart, our mind, and center, rebalance before we make decisions, before we react, yes, even before we speak. More often than now, we as people react too quickly, take actions that later we regret because we are hurt, or angered. Our task, our mission, our true actions should be step back, look at everything as a third party observer, go into the inner room, or perhaps our chapel, our bedroom, where ever we can be quiet, be reflective, to reconsider what we are planning. Well, he/she did this, said that, he/she deserves punishment. Ah, but he who is without ... let him/her throw the first stone (Jesus – John 8:7) We don't have to take on the responsibility of punishing, of correcting, as Karma, that is what karma is all about, the actions will create reactions, will bring repercussions. We just have to keep doing the right thing, no matter what others around us do. When we do the right thing, in our room, we can sleep at night, no matter what he/she, the world does, we won't be afraid, we won't have fear, and we will have peace.

Animal totem of the Day: Sea Anemone.

Sister Anemone is a sea fairy, a sea flower. She hides away in her room, of tide pools, where the sea opens doors to the Other side. Her medicine teaches us to open doors, but not to rush through with actions; not try to take actions quickly without thought without love, without heart first. Sister Anemone can expect new relationships, new events, both good and bad to come into our life. Her medicine reminds us to stop, enter into our room, and then take our dreams to manifestation.

Stone of the Day: Opal.
Gender: Female. Planet: Moon, Venus. Zodiac: Scorpio. Chakra: Throat, Heart. Deities: Shiva, Opal, Cardea, Venus.
Properties: Opal helps with our inner beauty, faithfulness, fidelity. Past lives are remembered, helps with creative visualization, emotional security, helps authors write, actors act, musicians create new songs. Carrying opal is thought by many to aid with eyesight!

Herb of the Day: Caraway (Carum carvi).
Gender: Masculine. Element: Air. Chakras: Throat, Solar Plexus. Planet: Mars, Mercury. Deities: Artemis, Mercury, Mars. Caraway seeds are used for Protection, Lust, Health, Anti-Theft, Mental Powers. Any object which holds some caraway seeds is theft-free. This herb helps promotes lust when baked into breads, cookies, or cakes. The seeds strengthen the memory.

Recipe of the Day: "*Caraway Cheese Ball*"
Ingredients:
¾ cup (8 ounce package) cream cheese softened
2 Tablespoons Dijon mustard
2 Tablespoons dry Sherry
1 teaspoon caraway seeds
2 Tablespoons vegetable oil
1 pound shredded Cheddar Cheese
3 tablespoons caraway seeds, for rolling
Directions:
Beat the cream cheese in a large bowl until fluffy and soft. Stir in the mustard, sherry, and 1 teaspoon of caraway seeds, mixing thoroughly. Beat in the Cheddar cheese and vegetable oil. Shape mixture into a ball and roll in the remaining 3 tablespoons of caraway seeds. Wrap coated ball in plastic and refrigerate until firm, at least 4 hours.
This recipe has prep time for 10 minutes. Ready in 4 hours - 10 minutes. Serve with wine and fruit for good news.

*This recipe was submitted to **allsrecipe.com** by jlamb36. Yet cheese balls are all over the cookbooks, so we can see that we* *can make varieties of this by instead of caraway – coat with nuts, or sesame seeds, sunflower seeds, the possibilities are endless.*

DAY 5:

"It's not that unusual When everything is beautiful It's just another ordinary miracle today The sky knows when it's time to snow Don't need to teach a seed to grow It's just another ordinary miracle today Life is like a gift they say Wrapped up for you every day. Open up and find a way To give some of your own Isn't it remarkable Like every time a raindrop falls It's just another ordinary miracle today Birds in winter have their fling Will always make it home by spring It's just another ordinary miracle today When you wake up every day Please don't throw your dreams away Hold them close to your heart 'Cause we're all a part of the ordinary miracle Ordinary miracle Do you want to see a miracle? It seems so exceptional The things just work out after all It's just another ordinary miracle today Sun comes up and shines so bright And disappears again at night It's just another ordinary miracle today It's just another ordinary miracle today" ~ Songwriters BALLARD, GLEN / STEWART, DAVID ALLAN

Curious, today I thought there is a miracle coming today. So many look at the life's path, the world right now, the country, even their own day in, day out lives, each one sure that nothing good is going to happen, that no miracles exist anymore. Curious, I thought about why we find it so hard to believe that miracles can happen to us. We do everything we can to throw our dreams away. We build up negativity in our mind, refusing to believe in the positive side of life, of the situation. We purposely do things to get revenge, to hurt, to pay back the very person we claim to love, or the job, the career we wanted so badly to build. We only think in this moment, not tomorrow, or even today's miracles, today's changes that are coming. We are so sure the visionary that tells us positive affirmations are WRONG, WRONG, or worse yet, trying to trick us. Curious, I wonder so strongly why we seem to want to believe the worse. Curious, I am so curious, that we seem to dwell in fear, doubt, worry, when every faith system known to man tells us not to worry. Every hair on our head is counted; the universe is set up to provide us our needs, our desires. Curious that we deny ourselves our miracles. Today I chose to believe again the fairies dance; the moon shines with love, the Sun smiles on us. Venus kissed our love, to bring the magick, the miracles in our lives.

Animal totem of the Day: Sea Urchin.
Sister Urchin teaches us to look closely at things in a different light. Under the surface, deep within, this totem is slow, methodical, tenacious, patience toward making the miracles, the impossible happen. Her tough exterior hides, but also protects her softness inside. Her medicine teaches us to not become hard inside as well trying to protect. Try to understand all sides of the story the situation with her teachings.

Stone of the Day: Black Tourmaline.
Gender: Male. Planet: Saturn. Chakras: Base Chakra. Zodiac: Capricorn. Element: Earth. Deities: Manat, Arcadia, Zeus. Properties: This stone repels and protects against negativity; brings energy to the physical well-being, vitality, emotional stability.

Herb of the Day: Cinnamon (Cinnamonum zeylanicum), aka sweet wood.
Gender: Masculine. Planet: Sun. Element: Fire. Deities: Venus, Aphrodite, Ra. Chakras: Sacral Chakra, Heart Chakra. Properties: He promotes spirituality, healing, power, lust, protection; can be empowered with tourmaline as well. This herb is used because of the high spirit vibrations with the use. Money spells get pepped up. Cinnamon is great for digestion, for energy boosts. He speeds up the metabolism.

Recipe of the Day: "*Cinnamon Rice*"
<u>Ingredients:</u>
1 cup uncooked rice
2 cups water
2 Tablespoons nonfat milk
5 tablespoons raisins
2 teaspoons margarine
½ teaspoon ground cinnamon
1 teaspoon sugar
<u>Directions:</u>
Bring rice, water, milk, raisins, and margarine to a boil in a saucepan over medium-high heat, stirring occasionally. Reduce heat to low, cover, and cook until liquid has absorbed and rice is tender, about 15 minutes. Mix together cinnamon and sugar, sprinkle over rice to serve.
Quick, easy, so good. Prep time is only 5 minutes; cooking time is 25 minutes, total time: 30 minutes.

Written and submitted on ***allsrecipe.com*** *by just "Dave". This is a great idea to add spice to a romantic dinner before love life.*

DAY 6:

"If you want to forget all your other troubles, wear too tight shoes." ~ The Houghton Line, November 1965

"If you can find a path with no obstacles, it probably doesn't lead anywhere." ~ Frank A. Clark

Everything is running smoothly so we think in our lives. Man, this is a breeze, where we finally have everything organized, on schedule, where we can breathe a little easy. Boom, the bottom falls out. Here we are, another obstacle. Where did that spring up from? Yet, we people are extremists. Instead of seeing this problem as a puzzle to show how smart we are in getting it fixed, or seeing where good changes are coming out of this situation, we go to the other end of despair. We sink down so far that we can't see round the bend. We often in our life's ups and downs act like we are already wearing our shoes too tight. The answer: take the shoes off. Yet in other situations, most often in love situations, that answer isn't the right one. We are so ready to be extremists, dumping this person because the relationship hit a wall, hit a hard problem, he/she is being distant, impossible to talk to, or hard headed. He/she is just as sure as we are that we are RIGHT! Now, Deb, if this was true love, or the right relationship, there wouldn't be any obstacles, no problems, all would be smooth sailing. Yet here, Mr. Frank A. Clark reminds us that if we find a path with no obstacles, the path leads to nowhere. We stay. We stay stuck where we are in this situation. We aren't married, or in a serious relationship. The relationship is where it has always been. The reason is we don't want to work at it, we don't want to face problems; we just want to sail smoothly. Change only comes with just that, change. Allow change. Allow obstacles. Take off the tight shoes, but keep the love.

Animal totem of the Day: Scorpion.

Scorpion is a transformer. Bringing change, his totem reminds us that change can be chaotic, or calm. His medicine tells us to make that decision. Bro scorpion meshes life and death, light and dark, rebirth from the endings. Changes come from the ending of the other way things were happening. Scorpion is strong, inspiring as rebirth comes from the ending. This totem helps by receiving spiritual messages.

Stone of the Day: Citrine.
Citrine is a variety of Quartz. Citrine is a 13th Anniversary gemstone. Gender: Male. Chakras: Sacral Chakra, Solar Plexus Chakra, Crown Chakra. Birthstone: November. Zodiac: Aries, Gemini, Leo, Libra. Planet: Jupiter. Element: Air. Deities: Aries, Athena. Properties: Citrine attracts wealth, prosperity, success. This stone raises self- esteem, confidence. An intellectual stone, it motivates intelligent actions, creativity. He releases depression, fears, anxiety, and balances chakras. Medically this reverses degenerative disease, stimulates digestion, spleen, blood.

Herb of the Day: Dill.
Gender: Masculine. Chakra: 4th Heart. Planet: Mercury. Element: Fire. Quality: Yang. Zodiac: Gemini. Powers: Protection, Money, Lust, Love. The use of dill in foods will help digestion, help relieve water retention, heals the colds. The use of dill pickles is thought to encourage romance after dinner.

Recipe of the Day: *"Glazed Dill Carrots"*
Ingredients:
3 cups peeled, sliced carrots
2 tablespoons butter
2 tablespoons brown sugar
1-1/2 tablespoons fresh chopped dill
½ teaspoon salt
½ teaspoon black pepper
Directions:
Place carrots in a skillet and pour in just enough water to cover. Bring to a boil over medium heat; simmer until water has evaporated and the carrots are tender. Stir in butter, brown sugar, dill, salt, and pepper. Prep time 10 minutes, cook time 10 minutes. Done in 20 minutes.

Laurie Cotnoir designed this Maple dill dish. We thank her for sharing on ***allsrecipes.com****.*

DAY 7:

"Here comes the sun Here comes the sun, and I say It's all right Little darling It's been a long, cold lonely winter Little darling It feels like years since it's been here. Here comes the sun Here comes the sun, and I say It's all right Little darling The smiles returning to the faces Little darling It seems like years since it's been here. Here comes the sun Here comes the sun, and I say It's all right Sun, sun, sun, here it comes…… Little darling I feel that ice is slowly melting Little darling It seems like years since it's been clear Here comes the sun" ~ Songwriters LENNON/HARRISON/MCCARTNEY

This winter has been brutal. Wikipedia and Weather Channel state that this winter has been one of the worst. The most recorded low temperatures were in 1917, Sioux Falls had lowest of –36 and Niagara Falls froze so densely one could break the ice off. Our lives, too, often have winters such as this. We feel so cold; it is actually a physical pain. Yet here comes the sun. Father Sol comes closed to the Mother earth, to warm her up, to bring beauty, to bring joy back into our lives. This problem we have right now, this sadness, this heartache, will pass. The truth will come out. Like oil, in water, truth seems to separate out, making sure the light over comes the dark. We will see the truth, we will see the Sun, and we will see joy. Only when we refuse to give up the anger, the fear, the doubt, the bitterness, and the heartache will these problems linger on. Forgiveness - for ourselves especially but for the other person as well -is the only way to let us out of our prison of winter in our soul. As long as we hang on to the dark, we build the wall that finds the positive, the sun to get through to our soul. Our soul is like our universe. Let the dark go, let the sunshine in. Open our heart. Yes, there are times when we may get hurt. We all do at times, but we will let the sun shine in by throwing open the doors, the windows, the shades of dark.

Animal totem of the Day: Scallop.

Scallop lives in the water. Sister Scallop teaches us to balance our emotions, our spirituality with positive thoughts even in the roughest waters. Move with patience as this totem is slower than others. Her medicine shares movement by opening up all the mind, body and spirit to the light to the sun. She teaches us we must be open, ready to face whatever our path tosses us, taking advantage of the positive times, positive opportunities when each one comes. Scallop has a tendency to hide, so do not hide behind our walls.

Stone of the Day: Coral.
Coral is a 35th Anniversary gemstone. Gender: Masculine. Planet: Mars. Zodiac: Taurus, Pisces. Element: Fire. Deities: Opuhala, Vasilisa.

Herb of the Day: Fennel.
Gender: Masculine. Planets: Jupiter, Mercury, Venus. Elements: Fire, Air. Quality: Yang. Zodiac: Virgo, Libra. Months: August, September. Sabbat: Midsummer. Rune: Uruz, Inguz. Deities: Adonis, Dionysus, Promethus. Powers: The ability to end hexes, cast out demons, healing, love, draws money, gives protection. Medicinal uses include helping women increase milk when breast feeding. This herb reduces gas, cramps, as dill heals water retention.

Recipe of the Day: *"Fennel Veggie Soup"*
Ingredients:
¼ cup butter
5 fennel bulbs, trimmed and quartered
32 ounce container vegetable broth
Salt and pepper to taste
Directions:
Melt the butter in a large skillet over medium heat. Add the quartered fennel bulbs; cook and stir until golden brown, about 10 minutes. Pour in the broth, and simmer until fennel is tender, about 15 more minutes. Ladle into soup bowls, and season with salt and pepper. This takes 5 minutes of prep time, cooking time is 25 minutes. We can be eating dinner in 32 minutes.

*Found on **allsrecipe.com** , submitted by Adamgodes. Give it a try.*

DAY 8:

"The clock talked loud. I threw it away, it scared me what it talked." ~ Tillie Olsen, Tell Me a Riddle

"Time is on my side, yes it is. Time is on my side, yes it is. Now you all were saying that you want to be free But you'll come runnin' back (I said you would baby), You'll come runnin' back (like I told you so many times before), You'll come runnin' back to me. Time is on my side, yes it is. Time is on my side, yes it is. You're searching for good times but just wait and see, You'll come runnin' back (I said you would darling), You'll come runnin back (Spent the rest of life with ya baby), You'll come runnin' back to me." ~ Jerry Ragovey

The clock ticks loudly in the silent room. The quiet being so loud, the tension so sharp, the air could be cut like a knife. Everyone seems to be holding breaths waiting for someone, anyone to break the limbo, putting an end to the standoff we are facing in our lives, in our relationships. We are glad for the time spent waiting for the changes. Over time, all life changes, so as we look at the time, we know that no time is wasted as we all change during these times. The good news is that no time is wasted as spirit is moving during the hiatus, the slumber, the winter of our lives, leading into balance in relationships - in jobs, in business. The universe often asks us to wait, hurry up, and wait again. We stand in puzzled amazement as we rush to do the bidding of the spirit, yet we are told to wait. He/she, the career is our destiny, we are told this, yet here we are waiting, standing still. Yet the universe has a perfect plan to bring the dream alive, the dream, the hope, will come alive.

Animal totem of the Day: Scarab.

In ancient Egypt, Ra god of the Sun, and immortality calls on the scarab to remind us that resurrection comes after the slumber, the waiting. This beetle totem is like caterpillar, is the symbol put on the mummies, reminding of the new life coming through reincarnation. His medicine teaches us to pace through the wait times realizing that good things, good changes come to new beginnings with time.

Stone of the Day: Garnet.

Gender: Male. Chakras: Base Chakra, Heart Chakra. Birthstone: January. Zodiac: Aries, Leo, Virgo. Planet: Mars.

Element: Fire. Properties: Garnet is a stone of cleansing, re-energizes the chakras, the energies of our auras. The beautiful stone balances sex drive with love, devotion, spiritual connection. In magick, draws love, and passion. Wearing garnet will help speed up the metabolism, helping to lose weight quicker. Disorders of spine, bone, composition, purifies the heart, lungs and helps heal the immune system are some of its traits.

Herb of the Day: Fig.

Gender: Masculine. Planet: Venus, Jupiter. Element: Fire. Quality: Yang. Zodiac: Sagittarius. Day: Thursday. Sabbats: Samhain. Deities: Bacchus, Dionysus, Flora, Juno, Mars, Pluto, Pomona, Zeus, Isis. Powers: Divination, Fertility, Love. Theory states that figs are love fruits, bringing fidelity, children into the relationship. Medicinally figs are full of potassium. If we tire of our regular banana for this much needed mineral, eat some figs. Hearts are kept healthy, with lowered blood pressure, good circulation.

Recipe of the Day: *"Fig & Brie Crostini"*

Ingredients:

1 cup finely chopped dried figs
½ cup cider vinegar
¼ cup brown sugar
¼ cup minced white onions
½ teaspoon ginger
1 pinch garlic powder
1 pinch cayenne pepper
1 pinch ground cloves
1 pinch ground cinnamon
Crostini: 1 loaf French bread cut into 1 inch slices
Olive oil cooking spray
1 8 ounce round Brie Cheese – cut into bite size pieces
1 regular size Granny Smith apple – cut into match size pieces
1 Tablespoon oregano

Directions:

1. Combine figs, vinegar, brown sugar, onion, ginger, garlic powder, cayenne pepper, cloves, and cinnamon in a saucepan; simmer over low heat, stirring occasionally, until fig spread is reduced, about 30 minutes. Transfer fig spread to a bowl; cover with plastic wrap, and refrigerate- 8 hours to overnight.

2. Set oven rack about 6 inches from the heat source and preheat the oven's broiler.
3. Arrange bread slices on a baking sheet. Lightly spray both sides of each bread slice with olive oil cooking spray.
4. Bake bread slices under the broiler until toasted, about 2 minutes per side. Remove bread from oven and cool slightly, keeping broiler on.
5. Blend fig spread in a blender or food processor until pureed. Spread about 1 teaspoon fig spread onto each toasted bread slice; top with Brie cheese and apple pieces. Sprinkle each crostini with oregano.
6. Broil crostini in the preheated oven until Brie cheese is melted and browned, 1 to 2 minutes. The prep time on this is 35 minutes, cooking time 35 minutes, then serve in 8 hours! Wow, impress folks with this Greek dish.

As we can see, I use ***allsrecipe.com*** *for the original recipes. Shine them up a bit for my taste of the taste of the customer. Here we took Shannon McK's thoughts, made it our own.*

DAY 9:

"As a single footstep will not make a path on the earth, so a single thought will not make a pathway in the mind. To make a deep physical path, we walk again and again. To make a deep mental path, we must think over and over the kind of thoughts we wish to dominate our lives." ~ Henry David Thoreau

The beautiful elderly woman, regal in her wheelchair was ready when I got there. She had a heavier jacket on, her cell phone in her hand. No, she can't speak, but she can listen. She didn't want to miss a call while gone, just like we carry ours everywhere. That one small touch of normalcy can make our thoughts positive for the day, for the moment. Ah but I was 5 minutes early, so she pointed at the clock refusing to leave until she finished the show on the TV. So I laughed, stating I had to go sign her out anyway. By the time I got back to the door of her room at the nursing home, she had wheeled herself out to the hall, ready to go. For the last week, we had fought. She wanted to go home. Tears, signing (she knew blind/deaf sign language - I'm finally learning the basics), even pounding her fist on her wheel chair, I got the message she wanted to go home. I questioned if this was the right thing to do, but the days went by, she just got angrier at her path. So I told her Monday at 10:30 am I would pick her up, take her home. See, she hasn't been to her home, for over 2 ½ years - in July the time passed will be 3 years. Long years of not being able to speak, not able to take steps, her path has not been easy. Questioning the gods, I often cry after leaving her, as this woman of great faith, so much faith all her life, is on this path, this journey. She never smoked, drank alcohol, cheated, and was married to the same man for 62 years, no matter how ups and downs hit her. She followed her faith's rules, her heart good. Yet in her mind, she determined to have thoughts that were good, that were loving, not jealous, not selfish, but the staff says, "OH your mom is the sweet one." How inspiring. So yesterday with the help of 2 friends, we went to see her house, her home. She rolled around looking in every room, rolling her eyes at the spot in the wood floor where my dad had spilled some rubbing alcohol, then she looked at every picture, every thing. Then just as easily, ready to face her path, get back on the journey to recovery, we headed back. Miracles happen, as we were told she wouldn't recover her mind, yet she has. We were told she wouldn't ever speak, but she can say the word NO very well, yet Time has to be our friend. We can make time waiting our friend, thinking thoughts of positive thoughts, of love, of hope, or we can become bitter, angry at our path we have been given. Time is our friend, as in time all life changes, good things will come. My mother, my inspiration, time is on our side as we go this path determining for our thoughts to be strong, patient, of hope.

Animal totem of the Day: Snail.
Slow as Brother Snail. His totem is one of protective spirits. Snail's medicine teaches us to trust time, to learn to trust, in faith. Yet his hard shell reminds us to protect our hearts, our spirits from darkness creeping in. Protect the inner child that has complete faith. Present to the world a strong chin up attitude while keeping the heart soft with love.

Stone of the Day: Howlite.
Gender: female. Planet: Moon. Zodiac: Gemini. Element: Air. Chakra: 3rd eye, crown. Deities: Ganesha, Venus. This is a protective stone. A softer stone, the rock holds protection with a soft inside. It draws psychic abilities. Medically, it heals the nervous system, circulatory system.

Herb of the Day: Ginger.
Gender: Masculine. Planets: Mars, Moon, Sun. Element: Fire. Quality: Yang. Zodiac: Aries, Leo, Scorpio. Month: November. Day: Tuesday. Powers: Metaphysical properties: repelling negativity, energy healing, love, Lust, love, draws money. Medically: Ginger is good if we have lost our appetite. The use of ginger for nausea is well known in medical and alternative circles, cramps, joint aches, romance aphrodisiac! All around great herb for our diet.

Recipe of the Day: *"Ginger Swordfish"*
Ingredients:
¾ cups teriyaki sauce
2/3 cups dry sherry
4 teaspoons minced garlic
2 teaspoons minced fresh ginger root
1 teaspoon sesame oil
6 (6) ounce swordfish steaks

Directions:

1. In a large saucepan combine teriyaki sauce, sherry, garlic, ginger, and sesame oil. Bring to a boil. Set the marinade aside to cool for 10 minutes.
2. Place fish in a shallow baking dish. Pour 1/2 of the marinade over the fish. Flip the fish over and pour the remaining marinade on the fish. Coat entire fish with marinade. Refrigerate the fish for 1- 1/2 hours, turning the fish over often.
3. Grill the fish over medium-high heat for 4 minutes. Flip the fish over and grill it another 4 minutes. Fish should flake easily with a fork when done. Serve hot! This takes prep time of 5 minutes; refrigerate 1 -½ hours, cooking time: 15 minutes, total time 1- ½ hours!! Good stuff!

This is one that many restaurants, Asian cuisines use, but this one is attributed simply to "Jessie".

DAY 10:

"Happiness is never stopping to think if you are." ~ Palmer Sondreal

"Talkin' to myself and feeling old. Sometimes I'd like to quit; Nothing ever seems to fit; Hangin' around, nothing to do but frown; Rainy days and Mondays always get me down What I've got they used to call the blues: Nothin' is really wrong; Feelin' like I don't belong; Walkin' around, some kind of lonely clown; Rainy days and Mondays always get me down Funny, but it seems that I always wind up-a here with you; Nice to know somebody loves me. Funny, but it seems that it's the only thing to do: Run and find the one who loves me." ~ Paul Williams, Roger Nichols

Okay yes today is Monday. This is a glorious new beginning to the business part of our week. Sunday is meant to be a day of rest, although in this busy world, we often don't take the time we need to stop, feel the sun on our face. Yesterday I stopped by the lake. I walked with bread in hand to the side to feed the ducks, the swans, there in our city lake. I lifted my face to Father Sol with the tears running down my face, as I cried out for the people. So many hurting lives, so many in despair; yes still the old hippie, I asked please to save the world. In my You-Tube video, I played "In a distance, the gods are watching." Yet I stand before the universe the heavens sharing that we don't need help from a distance. We need help right here in the middle of the trenches, of our lives. The pain, yes, even a physical pain, right in the middle of our chest, hits like a clamp tightening around the heart, the lungs so we can't even breathe. We cry, we become angry, we plea with our hearts, we see others smile, play, laugh, yet we don't come to realize that each person carries a burden. So Monday comes, the rain comes, we call out, so we ask, let us be the person of love, of hope, of faith. Asreal, archangel of the water, of emotional and spiritual - open up the 3rd eye; let us see with vision and clarity the messages to send to me, so we can say that as the word is said, it will be. The dream will come, the sorrows will pass, but today in this moment, just let there be love, even if the loves comes from one like me.

Animal totem of the Day: Swan.
Brother Swan gracefully arches his neck bowing to his lady love. Swans mate for life; when losing one, he will mourn with a soulful cry not often heard. His totem is often one of quietness, as he is not an aggressive, but loving medicine. An ugly duckling, clumsy, often losing his way as he stumbled to maturity, his totem reminds us that no matter how ugly life gets, we are headed to the beauty, the grace, the wonder of love.

Stone of the Day: Jade.
Gender: Female. Chakras: Heart Chakra. Zodiac: Aries, Taurus, Gemini, Libra. Element: Earth. Planet: Moon. Deities: Coaticue, Aztec, Bona Dea. This lovely stone is an all-around stone. It brings money, success, good blessings, healing, fertility, prosperity.

Herb of the Day: Lavender.
Gender: Masculine. Planets: Mercury, Jupiter. Element: Air. Quality: Yang. Zodiac: Gemini, Cancer, Virgo, Aquarius. Day: Wednesday. Month: June. Sabbat: Midsummer. Rune: Fehu, Mannaz. Deities: Hecate, Saturn, Vestia. Metaphysical Powers: chastity, happiness, healing, calming, peace, prosperity, gentle sleep and dreams. Medically speaking this herb is great to calm frazzled nerves, help with relaxation of the nervous system, heart, and a nervous stomach; aids in sleep.

Recipe of the Day: *"Lavender Tea Bread"*
Ingredients:
¾ cup milk
3 tablespoon finely chopped fresh lavender
6 Tablespoons butter, softened
1 cup white sugar
2 eggs
2 cups all-purpose flour
1-½ teaspoons baking powder
¼ teaspoon salt
Directions
1. Preheat the oven to 325 degrees F (165 degrees C). Grease and flour a 9x5 inch loaf pan.
2. Combine the milk and lavender in a small saucepan over medium heat. Heat to a simmer, then remove from heat, and allow to cool slightly.

3. In a medium bowl, cream together the butter and sugar until smooth. Beat in the egg until the mixture is light and fluffy. Combine the flour, baking powder, and salt; stir into the creamed mixture alternately with the milk and lavender until just blended. Pour into the prepared pan.
4. Bake for 50 minutes in the preheated oven, or until a wooden pick inserted into the crown of the loaf comes out clean. Cool in the pan on a wire rack.
This recipe takes prep time: 15 minutes, cooking time: 50 minutes. Ready for High tea time!

Grammee's Goodies to Go uses lavender in quite a bit of recipes as it is really good for calming life. This one is shared on ***allsrecipes.com*** *by ShiKaria.*

DAY 11:

"Morning has broken, like the first morning. Blackbird has spoken, like the first bird. Praise for the singing, praise for the morning, Praise for them springing fresh from the Word."
~ Mark Stevens sung by Cat Stevens

The sun shines from behind clouds this am. The brightness of the morning floods over our inner spirit like the opening of the door to the heavens. We can see the fairies dancing in the stream of light flickering back, forth over the floor as the pups try to catch the sprites. The three amigos, my pups, sit at the door longing to go back out. We've had our run, I've a busy day, but the longing to just stay outside fills all of us. The freshly sown grass has a smell that makes us long for spring to hurry up, yet we have just a little more time left for the winter so a heavy blanket of golden straw holds the seed in place while it takes root. Blackbirds, crows, cardinals, blue jays even one sparrow light on it at time, but find it hard to reach through to the straw. Drawing my thoughts to life, we are in a winter of our lives. We long for the spring, with the fresh beginnings, yet here we sit, in limbo, nothing happening. Oh we planted the seeds, but now waiting for the new grass is hard. What if the blue jays get through the straw? What if the winds blow it all away? It cost a pretty penny, to get a beautiful lawn or relationship takes time, effort, everything we have, if we really desire this new choice. So while we wait, we learn to know that we are great. We are wonderful children of the universe. The whole of the universe is set up to give us what we need, what we want, what we desire. We put our love, our hope, our faith, our work, our efforts into this so we are the best thing that ever happened to this universe, this love, this desire. We are worth the blessings, we are worth the gains, and we are of the light. We are at the first morning; there are blessings to go out, to receive. Praise for the morning. Praise for the new day. Praise for this word, Praise for us as we are the light of this day.

Animal totem of the Day: Sparrow.

The master prophet, teacher, the son of this universe Jesus told us see the sparrow. She doesn't toil, she doesn't worry. She knows that she will be provided for, given her needs, her desires. Sister sparrow's totem reminds us to be happy as we will have our needs met. The female sparrow is brown, not too attractive, yet she receives with such gladness that even when the storms come, she is happy chirping a sweet glad song.

Stone of the Day: Lapis Lazuli.
Lapis Lazuli is a 9th Anniversary gemstone. Gender: Male. Chakras: Throat Chakra, Third Eye Chakra. Birthstone: December. Zodiac: Taurus, Sagittarius. Element: Water. Deities: Isis, Athena. This stone of protection guards against psychic attacks. Lapis lazuli releases stress, bringing deep peace. Gentle sleep and dreams, this stone is actually the first stone in the breastplate on the first high Priest. The stone boosts the immune system, lowering blood pressure, giving relaxation to the nervous system and heart.

Herb of the Day: Lime.
Gender: Masculine. Planets: Sun, Jupiter, Venus. Element: Fire. Quality: Yang. Zodiac: Leo, Aquarius, Pisces. Deities: Venus, Lada. Magickal powers: The lime draws energy, healing, health. He works with poppet magick well, as well as drawing the spirits. The brisk smell awakens the sleeping souls. Medically: Lime is a good source of Vitamin C, often ignored in the wake of orange or lemon. With honey, use in place of lemon. Helps with eyesight, stomach problems will settle easier with lime as lemon and orange are too acidic. A glass of lime water before meals will help us lose weight.

Recipe of the Day: "*Lime Biscuits*"
Ingredients:
¾ cup milk
1 Tablespoon fresh lime juice
2 cups all-purpose flour
1 tablespoon baking powder
1 lime, zested
1 teaspoon salt
½ teaspoon baking soda
10 tablespoons butter (real) cut into pieces
Directions:
1. Preheat oven to 400 degrees F (200 degrees C).
2. Mix milk and lime juice together in a bowl.
3. Whisk flour, baking powder, lime zest, salt, and baking soda together in a separate bowl; mix butter into flour mixture using two knives or a pastry blender until crumbly. Stir milk mixture into flour mixture until just moistened.

4. Transfer dough to a lightly floured work surface; knead a few times. Gently shape dough into a ¾-inch thick disc; cut into 12 biscuits using a 2 ½-inch floured cutter or the rim of a small juice glass. Reshape scraps as needed. Arrange biscuits on a baking sheet.
5. Bake in the preheated oven until golden, 15 to 20 minutes. This has a prep time of 20 minutes, cooking time 15 minutes for some lovely biscuits. Pour strawberries, whipped cream for a variation of strawberry shortcake.

*Great gift from **allsrecipes.com** given to everyone by simple name of "bringhomethebakin'".*

DAY 12:

"I waited for You today but You didn't show, no, no, no. I needed You today, so where did You go? You told me to call, said, You'd be there. And though I haven't seen You are You still there? I cried out with no reply and I can't feel You by my side So I'll hold tight to what I know, You're here and I'm never alone And though I cannot see You and I can't explain why Such a deep, deep reassurance, yeah You've placed in my life Oh, oh, we cannot separate, You're part of me And though You're invisible I'll trust the unseen I cried out with no reply and I can't feel You by my side So I'll hold tight to what I know, You're here and I'm never alone" ~ Songwriters BARLOW, REBECCA ELIZABETH MARIE/BARLOW, LAUREN ASHLEY NICOLE/BARLOW, ALYSSA KATHERINE/BARLOW, VINCENT ROBERT FRANCIS/BARLOW, MARY ANN

The day was sunny, so hot outside; an egg dropped broken on the hot sidewalk would have fried perfectly without the stove. Steam rose from the sewer ducts along the way, floating up under the dresses of office workers hurrying down the street to get in the cool air conditioning before makeup sweated completely off. Construction workers, without regulations hardhats on their head, t-shirts sleeves rolled up, tied sweatbands around their foreheads, sipping on sweet southern iced tea. My friend and I hurried as we scrambled to our car. Single women, we had dates that afternoon, dates for the first time in a while, to watch 2 musicians we had met play in the park! Stopping by a local carwash to make sure the car was tip top shape, we, of course, saw the big long line of cars, each patiently waiting. Finally our turn came to vacuum, so we would be next under the hoses, the steamers, the waxers at the auto wash. Here, our turn! I jumped in the driver's seat, pulled up. A car came flying in from the other side. A big man jumped out. Furious, no fear, I jumped out, getting in his face, sticking my finger in. I didn't see his size, I didn't see his bulk, I could only feel the injustice to the situation. Surprisingly, he didn't say a word, just jumped back in his car backed off, drove away. We pulled in. As we were washing the car, my friend said, "Good thing those two guys jumped in with you." There were no guys, I explained. She insisted she saw 2 guys. We searched around for them, but no one else saw any guys. (Excerpt from new expanded "Living with the Other Side, deborahmillspsychic 2013) People often wonder if we just have outrageous, wild imaginations, but this is not really my tale to tell, but my friend's. See, we often so often think we are alone. We feel so alone in our troubles, our problems we forget the universe, the gods, the powers that be, never leave us alone. We call for the help, we send our pleas, we get so angry, so bitter, so frustrated that we are not heard, but in the end, we are never alone. Just stand firm, hold to our expectations, we are never alone.

Animal totem of the Day: Seagull.
Soaring high above the problems, the rough waters, Sister Seagull teaches us to bridge the gap between the 2 worlds. Ancient messengers well known to the Celtic Druids, their culture, the ancestors of the ocean people, her medicine teaches us to trust the Other Side. Allowing ourselves to soar with the spirit within, and without, we learn to trust we are not alone, no matter how high we fly. This totem reminds us to go high to see all the sides, both positive and negative before making our choices.

Stone of the Day: Peridot.
Peridot is a 16th Anniversary gemstone. Gender: Female. Chakras: Solar Plexus Chakra, Heart Chakra. Birthstone: August. Zodiac: Gemini, Leo, Virgo, Scorpio, Sagittarius. Planet: Mercury. Element: Earth. Deities: Pele, Nuit, Venus, Mercury. Magickal powers: Peridot is beautiful to cleanse the earth with the green. She helps to handle toxins, jealousy, anger, bitterness, hatred, stress. Peridot starts to draw positive energies, joy, and confidence. Medically she strengthens the immune system, speeds metabolism to help us lose weight. Disorders of thyroid, heart, thymus, lungs, are helped by carrying the peridot.

Herb of the Day: Marjoram.
Gender: Masculine. Planets: Mercury, Mars. Element: Air. Quality: Yang. Month: January. Deities: Aphrodite, Venus. Magickal Powers: Theories are that we can get rid of hexes, negativity, entities to hurt us through the use of marjoram. Before taking off with Astral projection use a little marjoram. Chastity, health, love money and success. Medically we are looking at: better sleep, treating insomnia, calming anxiety.

Recipe of the Day: "*Salsa di Noci*"

Ingredients:

3 cups water, or as needed
1- 1/2 cups walnuts
2 cloves garlic, peeled
1 pinch sea salt
1 teaspoon chopped fresh marjoram
1 teaspoon chopped fresh thyme
1 teaspoon chopped fresh oregano
1/2 cup extra-virgin olive oil
3/4 cup heavy cream
1 cup finely grated Pecorino Romano cheese
Freshly ground black pepper to taste
Sea salt to taste
1 (16 ounce) box dry fettuccine pasta
1/2 bunch fresh chives, finely chopped

Directions:

1. Bring water to a boil in a small saucepan. Add walnuts and cook until they have softened slightly, about 5 minutes. Drain and set aside.
2. Combine garlic and 1 pinch sea salt in the bowl of a mortar and pestle. Grind to create a thick paste. Add walnuts, marjoram, thyme, and oregano. Grind until combined and slightly creamy, but still coarse.
3. Transfer the walnut mixture to a large bowl. Slowly whisk in olive oil to form a thick cream. Add heavy cream and Pecorino Romano cheese, whisk until combined. Season with black pepper and sea salt to taste.
4. Fill a large pot with lightly salted water and bring to a rolling boil. Stir in the fettuccine, return to a boil, and cook pasta over medium heat until cooked through but still firm to the bite, about 8 minutes. Drain.
5. Toss walnut sauce with pasta. Garnish with fresh chives and feta cheese. Takes prep time of 10 minutes, cooking time: 15 minutes. Ready to go in 25 minutes.

This wonder comes right to us from Marketchef.

DAY 13:
"You have brains in your head; you have feet in your shoes. You can go in any direction you chose." ~ Dr. Seuss

"The doors we open and close each day decide the lives we live." ~ Flora Whittemore

The new day is here. This is a day - thank the gods here - of sunshine. Father Sol shines down smiling on the earth as freshly sowed grass seed in my yard was watered by the tears of the heavens last night. Often times, we can look at the weather to see what the universe is feeling. We often talk about empathic being; we forget the universe is very empathic. Like a sponge, soaking up our energies, our very beings, the universe builds up the sadness, the darkness, the anger, the hurts of our souls, until finally the air, the earth, the water, the fire of lightning storms through raging against the dark. Yet, then we are sent the rainbow, the sun, and the warm winds of tropical lands far away. The universe reminds us that our lives are much like this. We have choices to choose. Not of free will, but how to handle the days we meet. We can choose to let the darkness cover our decisions, our minds, and our souls. We can choose to see the positive side, letting light shine in. With choosing happiness for our path as we are today, we allow the full light to shine with light we can find answers. Wallowing in bitterness, hate, anger, we cannot see how things can become the rainbow after the storm. We can only continue the storm. The new day is here. We can go toward the light, or we can stay in the darkness. We can choose.

Animal totem of the Day: Salmon.
Sister Salmon battles the current. She is heading upstream to where she lays her eggs to bear the new salmon to be born. She is very diligent. We used to live near the salmon run. Most salmon kept fighting the current, pushing her way up the run. Some got hung up in the rocks, often times if we were there, we would lift her over so she could keep going. This is why salmon is a symbol of wisdom, of strength. She knows when, where to get help bearing the burden. Her medicine never gives up, the totem keeps going.

Stone of the Day: Onyx.

Gender: Feminine. Onyx is a 7th Anniversary gemstone. Zodiac: Gemini, Leo. Element: Earth. Chakra: Base, Heart. Planet: Earth, Mercury. Deities: Freya, Sin, Antu, Venus. Black onyx is a protective stone, healing the negative energies, repelling any darkness that tries to overtake the situation. Medically the onyx helps heal the heart, blood disorders, strengthens bones and joints.

Herb of the Day: Mint.

Gender: Masculine. Planet: Venus, Jupiter, Mercury. Element: Air. Quality: Yang. Zodiac: Libra. Month: May. Deities: Dis, Hecate, Pluto. Magickal Powers: Mint's zingy smell and taste brings about quick Mental Powers, enthusiasm, power. Like its name for the place we make money, mint used in candles, in foods, draws money toward us. Lusty, luscious, the taste of mint brings a zing, a zest to life. Medicinally the mint is good to bring calm nerves, dispels depressions, and helps to bring high energy levels.

Recipe of the Day: *"Cream Cheese Mint Candy"*

Ingredients:

1 (3 ounce) package cream cheese, softened
1 tablespoon butter, softened (real butter)
3 cups confectioner's sugar
2 drops peppermint oil
Any color food coloring paste (optional)

Directions:

1. In a large bowl, combine cream cheese, butter, and confectioner's sugar. Mix in peppermint oil. Color as desired with food coloring paste, or leave white.
2. Roll mixture into small balls, and place on waxed paper. Flatten with a fork dipped in confectioner's sugar. Let dry for about 2 hours on waxed paper, then freeze or refrigerate.

Takes prep time of 30 minutes, ready to serve in 2-½ hours. No cooking here my friends!

We love these little candies, for a baby shower, or bridal party especially. Shared by "Diane" on ***allsrecipe.com****. Of course for variations instead of peppermint, we can have spearmint, wintergreen, vanilla - the possibilities go on.*

DAY 14:

"From a distance, there is harmony, And it echoes through the land. It's the voice of hope, it's the voice of peace, It's the voice of every man. From a distance we all have enough, And no one is in need. And there are no guns, no bombs, and no disease, No hungry mouths to feed. From a distance we are instruments Marching in a common band. Playing songs of hope, playing songs of peace. They're the songs of every man. God is watching us. God is watching us. God is watching us from a distance." ~ Julie Gold

"Make me an instrument of Your peace; Where there is hatred, let me sow love; Where there is injury, pardon; Where there is error, truth; Where there is doubt, faith; Where there is despair, hope; Where there is darkness, light; And where there is sadness, joy. O Divine Master, Grant that I may not so much seek To be consoled as to console; To be understood as to understand; To be loved as to love. For it is in giving that we receive; it is in pardoning that we are pardoned" ~ (widely but erroneously attributed to the 13th-century saint Francis of Assisi. The prayer in its present form cannot be traced back further than 1912, when it was printed in Paris in French, in a small spiritual magazine called La Clochette (The Little Bell), published by La Ligue de la Sainte-Messe (The Holy Mass League). The author's name was not given, although it may have been the founder of La Ligue, Fr. Esther Bouquerel.)

The gods have looked down on the cold hard world, renewing much of the Mother Earth with a touch of warmth to show us that somewhere, something more has us in mind. Somewhere, something more than mere humans is watching, waiting, knowing the exact right moment to bring peace, comfort, and joy into our lives, into our dreams. See, we all have burdens to bear, crosses to carry, but as humans, we find our reality is right now in this moment. Blink our eyes; this moment is done – gone, only HOW we reacted to this moment lingers to affect our future, our inner peace. We allow the burdens to get us down, our support group, family, friends tell us we are crazy to continue to believe. Yet our hearts refuse to let go! How wondrous our thoughts, our own faith must be to give us the gift of hanging on, in believing when we can no longer "see" to believe. I am often amazed at the inner strength in people as every day I try to be an instrument to help each one continue on. I do not create this desire, create the ability to go on, but am the instrument to lift up one more day when we lose sight of the vision, and we are weary of the dream as there seems to be no end. What a blessing we have to be an instrument to continue to affirm with faith, a vessel of spirit to continue to ask of the heavens, to petition the gods, to be a part of the manifestation of the dreams. In a distance, not too far over the horizon, we are being watched, loved, taken care of, in all ways.

Animal totem of the Day: Salamander.
Sister Salamander slips out from the dark hidden rock where she hid from the burdens; her appearance heralding transformation. Assistance from something more, something out there, comes from unexpected sources, unique ways, often mysterious ways, that we cannot see coming. Being in harmony with the universe is her medicine; the calling of all the children of the universe. She is the key to the successful changes, successful transformation bringing answers, solutions.

Stone of the Day: Moonstone.
Moonstone is a 3rd Anniversary gemstone. Gender: Feminine. Chakras: Third Eye Chakra, Solar Plexus Chakra. Birthstone: June. Zodiac: Cancer, Libra, Scorpio. Planet: Moon. Element: Water. Deities: Artemis, Athena. Magickal properties of the moonstone show us new beginnings. Moonstone – lady of the moon – is a stone for spiritual growth, spiritual strength. She heals the inner emotional stability, relieving stress. Psychics most often love moonstone as the stone opens the door to the Other Side. Medicinally speaking, moonstone will help our digestive tract; she eliminates toxins, helps with water retention. She is a good blood purifier.

Herb of the Day: Nutmeg.
Gender: Masculine. Planets: Jupiter, Moon, Uranus. Element: Fire. Quality: Yang. Zodiac: Leo, Sagittarius, Pisces. Day: Thursday. Month: November. Magickal Powers: The Old Craft has taught us that nutmeg will help with divination skills, energy fields, vibrations, and the powers of the spirits. Nutmeg will keep him/her faithful so eat lots of it. Medicinally we are looking at nutmeg to help with the digestive tract running smoothly. In Ancient Egypt the wise ones used nutmeg to stimulate the brain. Used for pain relief, as well as indigestion,

nutmeg is a good tool to use in our foods. A teaspoon in milk at night helps us sleep.

Recipe of the Day: "*Nutmeg Mushrooms*"

Ingredients:

1 pound fresh mushrooms
¾ cup dry white wine
1 tablespoon ground nutmeg
1 teaspoon salt

Directions:

1. Clean and slice mushrooms.
2. Combine all ingredients in a skillet and cook over medium heat until the wine comes to a boil. Reduce heat to low and cook until mushrooms are tender. Remove from heat and serve while hot. Prep time is only 5 minutes, cooking time only 10; we are ready to eat in 15 minutes.

*Who would have thought nutmeg in mushrooms? But Lorena Maples did, then added the original thoughts to **allsrecipe.com**.*

DAY 15:

"If we have no peace, it is because we have forgotten that we belong to each other." ~ Mother Teresa

"Peace cannot be achieved through violence; it can only be attained through understanding." ~ Ralph Waldo Emerson

The battle raged on. From the news, we could see the devastation that the fires, the shots, the rioters continued to keep up the fight. Living in Michigan during the Detroit riots 1967 was a scary time. People were even destroying the very people's home, shops, possessions that the whole fight started for anyway. The fight for the loved ones, the children tore through the ghettos, on to the suburbs, on even to the rural areas, leaving only devastation in our wake. Many times this is how we try to "fix" our relationships. We break it off, taking a break, walking away from our dream, in anger, yelling, saying bitter hateful words that destroy just as quickly, as easily as the fires of Detroit 1967. What fire destroys can often be rebuilt, sometimes better than before with new counters, new walls, fresh paint. Yet our words, our hurts often linger on, sometimes for years as we replay these scenes over, over in our minds. We find no peace as we continue to overthink, over play, hit the rewind button so many times, that in actuality we are not even remembering events as really happened to us. We also have a tendency to be about "me". No it is not fair, we are always the forgiving one, we are always the giver, and we are always the strong one. No, it is not just we are the one who has to keep trying. Yet we have to remember we belong to others, we belong to the universe. We are important children of the universe. What we do, affects everyone around us, in some small or big way every day. When we do the right thing, we have peace in our heart. Even if no one else does the right thing, we can sleep at night, knowing we did our best to give a little slice of peace to the world.

Animal totem of the Day: Sand Dollar.

Sister Sand Dollar we often don't realize is a living animal. Her actions are full of coordination, motivation. She holds her rigid exterior, but her medicine reminds us that constant change comes, in accepting change, we have freedom. Spiritual tests come. Handling this in peace, with love, her totem reminds us to burrow deep within our soul, our heart, our dreams, our love to be guided to right actions.

Stone of the Day: Malachite.
Gender: Masculine. Chakras: Heart Chakra, Throat Chakra. Zodiac: Libra, Scorpio, Capricorn. Planet: Venus. Element: Earth. Deities: Freya, Hathor, Juno, Venus. Magickal properties tell us to use malachite to keep our money in our pocket; this is a protective stone, protecting our prosperity, our needs being met. Medically we know that malachite will balance depression, moods. He lowers blood pressure, heals swollen joints. Women should carry malachite to keep hormones balanced.

Herb of the Day: Orange.
Gender: Masculine. Planets: Sun, Neptune, Venus. Element: Fire. Quality: Yang. Zodiac: Leo. Day: Sunday. Month: August. Deities: Hera, Zeus. Magickal powers are powers of fidelity, chastity. Orange will bring good energy, blessings into poppets adding joy, love. Medically we know of vitamin C, potassium, lowering cholesterol, blood pressure, heightens energy. OJ will help with blood sugar issues.

Recipe of the Day: *"Orange Hummus"*
Ingredients:
2 cups canned garbanzo beans, drained
1/3 cup tahini (sesame-seed paste)
3 tablespoons SMUCKER'S® Sweet Orange Low Sugar Marmalade
3 tablespoons extra-virgin olive oil
1 teaspoon minced garlic
1/8 teaspoon ground cumin
Directions:
1. Place all ingredients in blender or food processor and process on slow to medium speed until all ingredients are pureed.
2. Cover and refrigerate for several hours to allow flavors to blend.
3. Remove from refrigerator 15 to 30 minutes before serving.
4. Drizzle with additional olive oil if desired. Serve with pita chips, sesame crackers or cut fresh vegetables.
Prep time is only 5 minutes. Then serve! Everyone will love this!
Smuckers the jam, jelly company offered this one up. Who's going to walk away from this? Healthy and delicious.

DAY 16:

"If you are going through hell, keep going." ~ Winston Churchill

"What is hell? I maintain that it is the suffering of being unable to love." ~ Fyodor Dostoyevsky, The Brothers Karamazov

The last month has been really rough for most of us here in the States. Cold, Cold, weather, snow, ice, traffic, both air, automobile has had us stopped in our tracks. Even emotions, others around us, seem to let the cold enter into the inner being, reaching the soul where we keep seeking warmth, heat, a way out of the hell we have been living. We want to stop. We want to quit. We want to quit feeling beat up, every day, yes, every day, putting out yet another fire, hitting another crisis, yet again another chaos, yes another hell. There are some schools of thought that there is no hell after death, as death is a reward, but that we just keep coming back here to this plane, this spiritual soul reliving over, over again until we reach nirvana or perfect right. So we get up every day, we do all the right rituals, the prayers, the giving thanks for our day, while inside we keep dying just a little more. We seek answers from every portal, every faith system, every walk of life, but never seem to get the relief, the answers we are seeking. Our questions are always why we are going through the battles. Once years ago, I asked a very wise man, my mentor, why. His calm almost cocky response was, "Why Not". See, his belief is that those of us in the light are trusted to keep trying to do the right thing. That through the heartaches and the battles we learn how to better battle the next one; and to actually help others to the light as well. Fair? Oh no. Good, oh yes. Do we have to be perfect? Oh no. Jacob, later called the Father of Israel, stole; yes he stole his older brother's birthright. So he ran for his very life as Esau was going to kill him. As he ran away into the night, soon his travels wore him out. During the night, the angel visited him to give him a message. Jacob grabbed hold of the angel, said bless me, and held on. He actually battled the angel, winning his blessing. This Judaism history shows us that every day we battle to achieve our blessings. We just need to hold on.

Animal totem of the Day: Raven.

Sister Raven brings the mysteries of the dark into the light. Magick comes in, joining with the will, intentions we have to achieve our dreams. Her medicine reminds us to go into our darkness, win over the conflicts which fear, doubt, anger, and bitterness instill in us, and fly away into the light. This brings our healing, our blessings, and our miracles to us.

Stone of the Day: Fluorite.
Gender: feminine. Chakras: Heart Chakra, Throat Chakra, Third Eye Chakra. Zodiac: Capricorn, Pisces. Element: Air, Water. Planet: Mercury, Mars. Deities: Horus. Magickal properties are the using of fluorite to heal - cleansing, balancing and centering our chakras, our auras; draws money and success as well. In the medical way, we can carry fluorite, and heal our immune and nervous system.

Herb of the Day: Rose.
Gender: Feminine. Planet: Venus. Element: Water. Quality: Yin. Zodiac: Taurus, Libra. Day: Friday, Tuesday, Monday. Month: May. Sabbat: Stara, Beltaine, Midsummer, Mabon. Deities: Aphrodite, Aurora, Chloris, Cupid, Demeter, Erato, Eros, Flora, Hathor, Isis, Venus, Adonis, Hulda, Harpocrates. Magickal Powers: we are well aware that roses bring and encourage love, healing to protect romance, passion. Rose will draw our psychic powers out. Medicinally surprisingly people do not realize that roses have 10 times the vitamin C of an orange. Rose tea will relax, yet bring energy.

Recipe of the Day: *"Cardamom Rose Merlngues"*
Ingredients:
2 egg whites
1/4 teaspoon cream of tartar
2/3 cup white sugar
1/4 cup water
2 teaspoons rose extract
1/4 teaspoon ground cardamom
1/8 teaspoon salt
1 drop red food coloring (optional)
Directions:
1. Preheat oven to 250 degrees F (120 degrees C). Line a baking sheet with parchment paper.
2. In a mixing bowl, beat egg whites and cream of tartar together with an electric mixer on high speed until the mixture forms stiff peaks.

3. Place sugar, water, rose extract, cardamom, salt, and food coloring in a saucepan, and bring to a simmer over low heat, stirring until the sugar has dissolved. Simmer the mixture for a minute or two, stirring constantly, and very slowly pour the syrup in a thin stream into the egg whites, beating constantly with electric mixer on high speed. Beat until the syrup is incorporated and the meringue is stiff and shiny.
4. Drop by spoonfuls or pipe into rosettes with a star tip onto the prepared baking sheet. These can be prepped in 15 minutes, and cooked in 1 hour 15 minutes.

My mother has made meringues all my life. We loved them. When she was having trouble eating, I started researching cardamom as it is good for helping loss of appetite. The rose is here is rich in Vitamin C. This variation is from **allsrecipes.com** *from chikalin. Remember Cardamom helps increase appetite for those who have trouble with depression loss of appetite, also increases sexual love.*

DAY 17:
"The most glorious moments in your life are not the so-called days of success, but rather those days when out of dejection and despair you feel rise in you a challenge to life, and the promise of future accomplishments." ~ Gustave Flaubert

"Today's accomplishments were yesterday's impossibilities." ~ Robert H. Schuller

The feeling of moving forward fills our soul with a sense of peace. In the midst of a waiting period, we get antsy, anxious, the more we wait, the more we feel almost itchy. Grass seems to be growing under our feet, while we are just standing still!!! We cannot accomplish anything by sitting, waiting. Yet others around us just don't seem to get that we are wasting time. We want that promotion like yesterday please, but the boss just doesn't seem to get off his/her tuff, to put the papers through. The bank told us that loan modification would work, but why oh why are we having to send yet another set of papers. Our most glorious days, the days when people see our strength, our spirit, most importantly our faith is the days when we know that although we, ourselves, are not moving, underneath the spiritual world has everything going. Much like electricity flowing into our Television, our lights, we cannot see this energy but we have lights so work is going on. Brother Turtle sits in one place, sunning on the rock for long periods of time. We turn our head for a minute; he is somewhere on down the path. His movements so slow we never see him moving, but we look away for a minute, he has chased a fly down the path. Little by little so slowly we don't see the movement, yet there he goes, on down the road! Life is like that so we can savor each moment, smell each rose, each lilac along the way, yet still find ourselves moving forward.

Animal totem of the Day: Tortoise, Turtle.
Brother Turtle has a hard shell, but very soft insides. He knows when to stop, hide away from the world to meditate, to ponder each situation to protect himself. Tortoise is one of the oldest ancient totems, with his medicine reminding us that slow, steady wins the prize. One would think of Bro Turtle as a water animal, but he is actually the oldest symbol for Mother Earth. His medicine reminds us to stay grounded balanced, to find

ourselves knowing that fast, quick, impulsive ways are not always the best ways.

Stone of the Day: Mother of Pearl.
Mother of Pearl is a 1st Anniversary gemstone. Gender: Female. Planet: Moon, Neptune. Zodiac: Pisces. Chakra: Heart, Solar Plexus. Deities: Maha- serisavati, Venus. Mother of pearl has a calming effect that brings the psychic, the spiritual and the healing to our lives; this stone helps heal the heart in love, and physically helps with heart issues.

Herb of the Day: Chamomile.
Gender: Masculine. Planet: Sun. Element: Water. Associated Deities: Cernunnos, Ra, Sun Gods. Magickal Powers: healing spirit, emotions energies, relaxation, will bring love, helps to cleanse. Medically: heals sleep patterns, relaxation, calms upset stomachs.

Recipe of the Day: *"Lemon Chamomile Bars"*
Ingredients:
1 cup (2 sticks) unsalted butter
1/2 cup sugar
1/4 teaspoon salt
Grated zest from 1 lemon
1 teaspoon loose chamomile tea
2-1/4 cups all-purpose flour
Directions:
Heat oven to 325° F. Combine the butter, sugar, and salt in a mixer and beat until light and fluffy. Blend in the lemon zest, loose tea, and flour until smooth. Press into an 8-inch square cake pan.
Bake 30 minutes or just until the shortbread begins to turn golden. Cut into 9 squares, then cut each square into 2 triangles.
Cool completely on a wire rack. Remove the shortbread cookies from the pan.
Prepping time is only 15 minutes, cooking time: 30. Total time: 45 minutes.

*This recipe was found and compiled from **allsrecipe.com** and from best **recipes.com** together.*

DAY 18:
"Sorrow makes us all children again - destroys all differences of intellect. The wisest know nothing." ~ Ralph Waldo Emerson

What can I say? As I ask spirit what to say today, Positive Pollyanna Deb struggles through the grief, the sadness, to find some words, some comfort as to why the gods would let this tragedy at Sandy Hook Elementary to happen. Yet here it is, once again a shattering of the evil that seemed to be permeating our world, as a domino effect, trickling down to hit all our lives. Yes, today we will mend fences with family, the loved ones who we have argued with, we have fought; we have shut out of our lives. Today we will be a little sweeter even to the stranger behind the counter at the grocery store. Yes, we will put our coffers into the charity bins, the Santas ringing bells on the street corners, but we still wonder if it is enough. I often talk about negativity, how it is an entity, a spirit that reaches out, much like a bad apple in a barrel with other apples will taint all the apples, so does the negativity that reaches out from one heart to another, passing to others like we pass a bad cold germs. The air becomes almost tangible, palpable with dark energy, with negativity, until even the weather such as Hurricane Katrina, Hurricane Sandy comes, Columbine, Sandy Hook hits us with full force. Today we will reach out with positive love to touch others, but we must continue to strive, (I know it is hard, our lives, our wait for our dreams are long and hard) but we must strive to send the positive light out to the world.

Animal totem of the Day: Monkey.
We love to watch the monkeys. Their long arms can reach up high; we watch them swing high into the trees where all of life, good and bad can be seen. Monkeys represent the difference of light and dark. Bro chimp represents the dark side of people, but teaches us the key is to live right, live positively, Monkey's funny antics divert us causing us to see no evil, hear no evil, speak no evil, but may blind us to the knowledge that we are drifting down into a dark place needing to pull up , pull out of the funk we are in, give positive affirmations, to know that although evil is there, the dark is there, we can always destroy it by keeping up our light.

Stone of the Day: Diamond.

Diamond is a 60th Anniversary gemstone. Gender: Masculine. Chakras: Crown Chakra. Birthstone: April. Zodiac: Aries, Taurus, Leo. Planet: Venus. Deities: Indra, Diana, Baja, Hephaestus. Magickal powers: The diamond is well known to be given in promise to marriage. This is because this is a hard strong stone of prosperity, abundance, fidelity, love. The powers of diamond are strong, giving spiritual strength to any, to all relationships. Medicinally diamond helps keep the blood flowing properly, purifying, cleansing toxins from the bloodstream, also balances our metabolism, helps us lose weight.

Herb of the Day: Oats (Avena sativa).

Gender: Feminine. Planet: Venus. Element: Earth. Chakras: Solar Plexus. Deities: Venus, Tara Earth Mother, Gai. Magickal powers: Oats are good for money drawing, prosperity, draws passion, romance. Medically oats are good for fiber, protein, helps with digestion.

Recipe of the Day: *"Oat Soup"*

Ingredients:

3 tablespoons olive oil
1 cup oats
5 large tomatoes, halved and sliced
1/3 cup onion, chopped
1 clove garlic, chopped
3 cups water, divided
1/2 bunch fresh cilantro
2 teaspoons chicken bouillon granules
1/2 teaspoon salt

Directions:

Heat a large deep skillet or Dutch oven over medium-low heat. Pour in the olive oil, and let it heat up. Add the oats; cook and stir until toasted.

In a blender or large food processor, combine the tomatoes, onion, garlic, 1 cup of water, and cilantro. Blend until smooth. Pour into the pan with the toasted oats. Stir in the remaining 2 cups of water, and bring to a boil. Mix in the salt and chicken bouillon. Cover, and simmer for 15 minutes. Enjoy hot or warm. We can prep this in 10 minutes, cook in 15; so in 25 minutes we are sitting down to a nice hearty meal.

AlejandraGomez is the originator of this posting on ***allsrecipe.com*** *.*

DAY 19:

"Create each day anew by clothing yourself with heaven and earth, bathing yourself with wisdom and love, and placing yourself in the heart of Mother Nature." ~ Morihei Ueshiba

Today is the day we put aside all of last year's mistakes. All his mistakes, her mistakes, our mistakes can be tossed aside, as we have the bright new year starting tomorrow to face with gladness. We can cry today, sobbing into our pillow, letting all of 2013 go. We can be thankful for every moment of sunshine, every smile, every hope that came our way, but the times we ached with loneliness, we hurt with every inch of our being over the troubles we had, we can let flow out to the universe as we start this new year. We can plan for greatness, we can plan for joy; we have a whole empty chapter ready for us to determine how we want to write these pages. Yes, we are all still waiting, waiting for that elusive dream to come alive. We can see the little seeds that we planted back in Sept. Oct, starting to take root. We won't see the bulbs we planted, the tulips, the iris peeking in until perhaps April or May, but in our relationships we can know that if this dream is in our heart it is for a reason, for a purpose, so we can have hope, have happiness.

Animal totem of the Day: Mockingbird.

Mockingbird is a bird that doesn't really have her own personality. She has inner gifts of being an empathic. She reminds us that who we associate with, is who our energies become. Her medicine reminds us to look at the heart of people, not the actions, or even words before making a decision. If we spend time with negative nellies, we will be negative no matter how hard we are trying to be an example to these people. Having money, a beautiful body doesn't mean the person's heart is good, that spirit walks with this person. Mockingbird sings the song of whatever bird is around her. She has a beautiful voice of her own, but mocks those around her. Her totem reminds us to sing our own sacred song, hold to our own dreams.

Stone of the Day: Pearl.

Pearl is a 30th Anniversary gemstone. Gender: Masculine. Chakras: Third Eye Chakra. Birthstone: June. Zodiac: Gemini, Cancer. Planet: Moon. Deities: Isis, Aphrodite, Freya, Venus, Lakshmi, Diana, Neptune and Poseidon. Magickal powers: pearl is good to ensure faith, purity, truth, commitment. Pearls bring focus to magickal rituals. Medically, carrying a pearl heals digestive disorders. This stone will help kidneys, as well as easing childbirth.

Herb of the Day: Sage (Salvia officinalis).
Gender: Masculine. Planet: Jupiter. Element: Air. Associated Deities: Consus, Jupiter, Zeus. Chakra: Throat, Solar Plexus. Magickal powers: Sage has been used for centuries to cleanse, clear, repel negativity, and/or demonic forces. Sage helps in wisdom, clarity drawing wishes. Medicinally sage helps the digestive tract cleanse, purifying from toxins.

Recipe of the Day: *"Creamed Onions and Sage"*
Ingredients:
24 small onions
10 fresh mushrooms, sliced
4 tablespoons butter
2 tablespoons all-purpose flour
2 cups whole milk or half-and-half
1 teaspoon salt
2 teaspoons dried sage
2 teaspoons lemon zest
2 teaspoons lemon juice
4 tablespoons chopped fresh parsley
2 pinches paprika
Directions:
1. Peel onions and trim slightly at the top and bottom. Boil the onions gently in salted water until tender (about 30 minutes).
2. Preheat oven to 350 degrees F (175 degrees C). Butter one shallow baking dish.
3. Sauté the sliced mushrooms in the butter or margarine. Stir in the flour. Stir in the half- and- half or milk, salt, sage, 1/2 of the lemon peel and all of the lemon juice. Cook, stirring over medium heat until sauce thickens.
4. Place the cooked onions in the prepared baking dish and pour the mushroom sauce over them.
5. Bake at 350 degrees F (175 degrees C) for about 20 minutes. Sprinkle the top with the chopped parsley, remaining lemon peel and paprika to taste.
We can prep this awesome side dish in 10 minutes, cook for 30 then 20. We can be eating in 1 hour.

I'm not a big fan of onions, but Erika Michael added this to ***allsrecipe.com*** *making me a believer.*

DAY 20:

"If you can find a path with no obstacles, it probably doesn't lead anywhere." ~ Frank A. Clark

The young woman sat before me crying. If it was meant to be, it would be easier she said. Yet, I know the easy things are most often like a gas fire. The gas burns off, the fire flame is gone. Relationships are like this. We are taking two unique personalities, joining these together, binding the two, there are bound to be some difficulties. In fact of truth, I have observed in over 50 years of studying people, the greatest love stories are not easy at all. Relationships, much like having money, much like our job, is a matter of push, pull , give, take, tears, laughter, joy and pain. We can take 2 steps forward, then feel as if we are going backwards 10. Most often though, we are lucky enough to find that we were simply standing still for a moment, getting a rest, learning some lessons, finding balance, waiting on the other to catch up. The Paths with no obstacles usually keep us staying stagnant. A stagnant pond usually stinks, so if there are no changes, no growth, our relationship will start stinking. There will be no growth without an obstacle to show us what needs to be changed. See, we so often get so distraught by an obstacle but if we didn't have any obstacles, we wouldn't change anything, we would continue to live in quiet desperation, without hope for something better. Welcome the obstacles as these will bring changes that we need to continue to move toward the dream, to happiness. We will find the path that leads to somewhere!

Animal totem of the Day: Stork.

We often think of stork as the one who brings us our babies. This is because stork totem reminds us that although there are obstacles in the waters, there are always new beginnings of a new day. Sister Stork is one of the most ancient symbols of new beginnings as she connects of emotion. The Goddess Juno adores this totem; Juno rules home, children, family, bringing blessings to the home. Stork dances in the water, can also stand on one foot. She brings balance while still opening up primal energies to begin a new project, relationship or job. She shows us there may be obstacles but still we can see hope.

Stone of the Day: Quartz.

Gender: Masculine. Chakras: Crown Chakra. Zodiac: All birth signs. Planet: Sun. Element: All (Earth/Fire/Air/Water). Deities: Hecate, Arcadia.

Herb of the Day: Jasmine (Jasminum officinale).

Gender: Feminine. Planet: Moon. Element: Water. Associated Deities: Artemis, Diana, Maternal aspects of the Goddess, Vishnu, Zeus. Magickal Powers include the ability to draw love, draw money, abundance in all areas. We can have prophetic dreams, with renewed relaxation. This herb helps to cleanse the aura. Medically speaking we are using jasmine much as we use chamomile as a sleep agent, for gentle dreams, to relax at night. This is an aphrodisiac for passion. An antiseptic can be made with this herb. With the relaxation, the flowering herb can calm nerves, be a good antidepressant.

Recipe of the Day: *"Sweet Jasmine Rice"*

Ingredients:

3 cups water
1 jasmine herbal tea bag
1 cube vegetable bouillon
1-1/2 cups uncooked brown rice
1 tablespoon butter
2 tablespoons chopped fresh cilantro

Directions:

Combine the 3 cups of water and the tea bag in a large saucepan; bring to a boil. Remove tea bag from boiling water. Stir rice and bouillon cube into the flavored water; return to a boil. Cover pan; reduce heat to low. Allow rice to steam until the water has been absorbed and the rice is tender, about 45 minutes. Remove from heat and let rest for 5 minutes. Fluff cooked rice with a fork, and stir in butter. Top rice with chopped cilantro. We only spend prep time 5 minutes; cooking time 50 minutes.

On Allsrecipe.com, we can find some variations. Two of them come from "Brian", and "darmstro67".

DAY 21:
Alice came to a fork in the road. "Which road do I take?" she asked. "Where do you want to go?" responded the Cheshire cat. "I don't know," Alice answered. "Then," said the cat, "it doesn't matter." ~Lewis Carroll, Alice in Wonderland

The lover came to the point where he had to make a choice in this relationship. The time the couple had been seeing each other had passed enough time, he should know whether this was enough to be long lasting, or if it was just time to let it go. This question should be easy, all it takes is love. If he loves his lady, this question wouldn't even come up, but here it is. As all the what ifs, why nots, the working, the faults he himself has, where does he want to go? So he allows his mind to take over, thinking way too much about something spirit has already set in place. We, ourselves, often see where spirit wants us to go, then we over think about it, not listening to the inner voices at all, but when our partner, our love of our life, isn't listening clearly we get mad, lose faith in the vision, not looking at all sides of the picture. Simply put, if all of us just listened to spirit every day, in every way all the time, there would be no problems. This will not happen. Somewhere along the path, we decide we know better than Great spirit about what is the best way to handle this, that we "see" that it should be done this way, we should go down that fork so that then when we are lost , we have to find our way back. At the fork, sit, listen, step back like a 3rd party observer, and then decide where we want to go.

Animal totem of the Day: Seagull.
In my dreams, I walked along the ocean. Seagulls flew over my head, landing without fear at my feet, hoping for a bite of whatever I was eating at that moment. Scattering bits of my sandwich, I watched the birds gobble realizing their message was a spiritual awakening. Long a symbol of the Celtic deities, returning back to the Druids, their medicine reminds us that the door between the spiritual world and this world is open to us. Seagulls know how to rise above the problems by giving over to Great Spirit then asking to be shown the right path. Seagull knows to look at all sides, his/her side of things, not just our own.

Stone of the Day: Kyanite.

Gender: Feminine. Chakra: Throat, Solar Plexus, Third eye. Zodiac: Aries, Taurus, Libra. Element: Air. Planet: Mercury, Jupiter. Deities: Sumerian god Ki, Diana. Magickal powers: Kyanite is all about meditation, connection, spiritual cleansing, healing. She helps us balance both our chakras and our auras. This stone's properties calm, relax, soothe our energies, our nerves. Encouraging all our spiritual gifts, the ability to "see" can be quite stimulating. Dream visions are answers. Medically, Kyanite helps to heal the urogenital system, adrenal glands. Sore throat? Carry some Kyanite. High blood pressure? This stone will carry it down. Kyanite can help us relieve pain.

Herb of the Day: Comfrey.

Gender: Feminine. Planet: Saturn. Element: Water. Chakra: Throat, Crown. Deities: Odin, Loki, Frigg, Hecate the Crone. Magickal powers with comfrey bring us safe traveling, drawing money toward us, and bringing wisdom. Medically the uses for comfrey have been known to help us, slow down bleeding from a cut, aiding colds, healing burns, bites, rashes, sunburn.

Recipe of the Day: *"Comfrey Chicken Soup"*

Ingredients:

2 boiled chicken breasts - diced pieces
1 onion, sliced
1 tablespoon butter
1 large potato, peeled and diced
4 cups finely chopped, tender young comfrey leaves (use only fresh very young tender comfrey)
2 cups stock (vegetable, chicken or beef)
½ cup milk
Marmite or soy sauce to taste
Salt and pepper to taste

Directions:

Cook the chicken breast and sliced onion gently in butter in a large saucepan until soft.
Add potato and sauté.
Add comfrey and sauté all together for several minutes.
Add stock, bring to boil and then simmer gently until vegetables are tender.
Mash potatoes with a potato masher or if you prefer a smooth consistency blend in a blender.

Heat the milk and add to the soup.
Season to taste with marmite (or soy sauce), and salt and pepper.
Garnish with chopped parsley and serve with toast.

This recipe I've learned over the years from various different people. Recently a waitress at a restaurant and I were talking about the benefits of comfrey. I didn't catch her name, but we just chitchatted about what all we could add to this recipe.

DAY 22:
"There is no such thing as can't, only won't. If you're qualified, all it takes is a burning desire to accomplish, to make a change. Go forward, go backward. Whatever it takes! .... It all comes from your mind. When we do the impossible we realize we are special people." ~ Jan Ashford – author

Everyone knows I believe the impossible can be done. Through lives of many greats, we see things done that were called crazy, called impossible, called dumb to keep trying. Having faith in our dreams, what we believe that higher power has told us is not dumb but actual pretty smart. It's going to happen anyway because Higher Power never fails. So when we are sad, or we start doing things to help prove we are not dumb enough to believe it, we leave ourselves open to so many dark, so much negative junk in our lives , we think Higher power has forgotten us. He/ she hasn't forgotten us, we've forgotten how powerful the most high is, how smart, how good! Nothing that we can dream up is impossible. If we can think it, it can be done. Thankfully we have something more out there to help us, and then we will realize just how smart, how special we are.

Animal totem: Otter.
This morning on GMA the reporter told about otters attacking people. Something must be really wrong for these delightful animals to take aggressive stance. They must really want to remind us of their totem. If an Otter has entered your life, it may be time to find some play time in your life, to awaken your inner child. Allow events to unfold naturally in your life. Be careful not to hang on the material things in your life that bind you or become a burden. Become Otter and move gently into the river of life.

Stone of the Day: Lodestone.
Gender: Masculine. Chakras: Base Chakra. Zodiac: Aries, Virgo, Capricorn, Aquarius. Element: Earth. Planets: Earth, Moon. Deities: Aries, Venus, Mercury, Gia. Magickal powers: This stone is also called magnetite which is highly magnetic. This will help balance everything: chakras, auras, physical body, vibes, which will help ground, center and balance. It draws telepathy, meditation, visualization. Magnetite attracts love, taking away the fear, anger, grief out of the situation. Medically is anti – inflammatory, relieving muscles aches, joint

pains. This stone balances all the organs. This stone should never be worn by women who are pregnant, people with pacemakers, and/or defibrillators.

Herb of the Day: Parsley.
Gender: Masculine. Planet: Mercury. Element: Air. Chakras: Throat, Solar Plexus. Deities: Aries, Mercury, Athena. Magickal Powers: draws money, encourages passion, excitement, love. Medicinally we use this herb as a treatment for cramps, both menstrual, muscle cramps. Aids in healing joint pain; arthritis. Externally make a nice paste to heal insect bites, bee stings, draws out pain in sprains.

Recipe of the Day: "*Neptune's Delight*"
<u>Ingredients:</u>
3 tablespoons butter
¼ cup all-purpose flour
2 cups heavy cream, divided
2 ounces freshly grated Parmesan cheese
2 tablespoons dry sherry
½ teaspoon paprika
2 cups cooked tuna
2 cups cooked crabmeat
1 cup peeled cooked shrimp
5- ½ cups garlic-flavored croutons
¼ cup fresh parsley
4 tablespoons melted butter
<u>Directions:</u>
1. Preheat oven to 350 degrees F (175 degrees C).
2. In a large saucepan over medium heat, melt 3 tablespoons of butter. Remove from heat and whisk in flour. Pour in ½ cup of heavy cream and whisk well, return to heat.
3. Add cheese and stir until creamy. Remove from heat and pour in remaining cream. Stir in sherry, paprika, crabmeat, tuna and shrimp. Spoon mixture into 6 large individual ramekins or bowls.
4. In a food processor or blender, blend together croutons and parsley. Top each filled ramekin with crouton mixture. Drizzle melted butter over the top.
5. Bake in preheated oven for 20 minutes or until top is browned and bubbly.
The prep time for this is quick, only 5 minutes, and the cook time 20 so we are eating a nice seafood dinner in 25 minutes.

This delight is attributed on Allsrecipe.com by DoreenB but she calls it Ann's Neptune Delight so we can't give credit to where credit is due.

DAY 23:
"Be bold, be bold, and everywhere be bold." ~ Edmund Spenser

The earth is green today. The sun is warm, full of light. We walk out into the bright fresh morning ready to face our day. Yesterday's problems still linger around us. Fear of what will come this day takes over before we even get started. We are timid. We are insecure because past history has shown us nothing good. Today; though as we start out this beautiful morning, we know that we can feel positive that changes will come. We are bold. We can stretch ourselves past the fear we feel, past the door slammed shut, move into the path with grace, hope, positivity. Fear is our worst enemy. Fear paralyzes us. We do don't want to fail that we are afraid to make any move at all. Remember too, that, sitting still, saying our prayers, meditations, our daily rituals, we are taking some action. In putting our faith, our trust in a power Higher than ourselves, we are being bolder than we ever have been. Times have been hard. Nothing, yes, nothing has worked out as we thought, how we thought, WHEN we thought. We doubt not only if there is a spiritual world out there at all, but if we are even considered, even remembered. We feel forsaken. We feel lost. WE want to do something, anything. We trust "me". Be bold today. Trust, even, when there seems no reason to trust, be bold to trust. In every way, every time, be bold.

Animal totems: Scrub Jay.
Today I just looked up animal totems for boldness. Scrub Jay popped up. Not blue jay, which we know can be quite the bully. Blue jay will run others birds off from the food, the trees in his quest to be the most powerful. Scrub Jay brings memories, allowing feelings of guilt with joy at memories. This totem shows balance in boldness with a heart-felt compassion not seen by blue jay. There is great potential in this bird's boldness, bringing new perspectives, a different side or look to things then what we may be seeing. Scrub Jay investigates all sides, intellectually finding the connection, seeing that time helps us learn and grow spiritually. We may think we've "got this" spiritual thing down, we KNOW it all, but this scrub jay shows us we still have a lot to learn.

Stone of the Day: Sapphire.
Sapphire is a 45th Anniversary gemstone. Gender: Masculine. Chakras: Throat, Base. Birthstone: September. Zodiac: Virgo, Libra, Sagittarius. Planet: Saturn. Element: Water. Deities: Jupiter, Juterna, Zeus. Magickal powers: Sapphire is known as the wisdom stone, brought into rites for clarity, psychic healing, and knowledge. He keeps the clutter, the confusion out of readings. Medically we see sapphire treating blood disorders, stopping bleeding when we get cut.

Herb of the Day: Sunflower.
Gender: Masculine. Planet: Sun. Element: Fire. Chakras: Base, Sacral, Heart. Deities: Ra, Hecate, Tara. Magickal powers: opens the door way to love energies, brings good news blessings. Eating the seeds will increase fertility. Medically: a good vegetable source of fiber, protein.

Recipe of the Day: *"Sunflower Soy Spread"*
Ingredients:
2 cups sunflower seeds
½ cup tahini
¼ cup lemon juice
1 clove garlic, minced
2 tablespoons soy sauce
1 stalk celery, finely chopped
1 tablespoon minced onion
2 cups sliced grapes
½ cup water
Directions:
1. Toast seeds in a frying pan over medium heat for 8 to 10 minutes stirring non-stop, until lightly browned.
2. Transfer the hot seeds to a bowl and mix well with tahini, stirring well to coat all seeds. Spread seeds out in a single layer and cool to room temperature.
3. While cooling, combine juice and garlic in a small bowl. Set aside.
4. Put seeds in food processor or hand held blender along with the juice mixture, soy sauce, celery, minced onion .grapes and water; blend until the mixture is fairly fine. Cover and refrigerate if not using the spread within 15 minutes. If spread firms up, mix in a tablespoon of water.
We prep this dip spread in 15 minutes. No cook.

Soy is another healthy downright good food for you I'm not crazy about but I tried Krazykat's recipe she submitted to **allsrecipe.com** *. It's delish!*

DAY 24:

"The purpose of learning is growth, and our minds, unlike our bodies, can continue growing as we continue to live."
~ Mortimer Adler Smile

I don't want to do this anymore. We all have said this about our job, our relationship, even the dreaded word, "exercise". We have talents, great talents; each person has talents we know. Even great singers, actors, performers sometimes just want to run away. The key thing is we all need this solitude time. We all need a chance to stop, go into our inner peaceful place. Yet most of us are afraid of doing just this release. We need time to think without noise, without people yapping at us. The truth is in fact, so does he/she need that time. We are so focused on our fears, on our goals, on the what ifs and why nots, we forget to stop, reflect, renew, restore. We can try very hard to keep everything the same. Some of us even love the drama, the chaos, but then we are yelling at the universe, I don't want to do this anymore. I want to stop!! I want to get off. We don't have that option. We just keep on growing, keep on learning, as we continue to live on this plane.

Animal totem of the Day: Bear.

Bro Bear is smart. He learns how to absorb everything in a few months, then go into hibernation, to dream, to think, to realize where his strengths lie, where he needs to grow. Bro Bear is never aggressive unless he needs to protect, hungry, or feels a danger nearby, then he can run quick fast, scale any tree, or mountain. His medicine is strength, which he gains in spending much time alone in hibernation; growth.

Stone of the Day: Sunstone, or Feldspar.

Gender: Male. Chakras: Sacral Chakra, Solar Plexus Chakra. Zodiac: Leo, Libra. Element: Fire, Air. Deities: Ra, Aries, Athena, Sol. This is sunstone, named as for Father Sol the Sun. He is linked to good blessings, good fortune. Clearing, balancing, energies all the chakras, this stone helps us to stay in a good mood. Being able to heighten our intuition, we can realize that with carrying this stone, the doorways to the Other World are brightened so we can have enlightenment. Medicinally this stone will help with depression, stimulates our ability to gain confidence, independence, and love. Some theories tell us that sunstone treats sore throats, reduce tension.

Herb of the Day: Saffron.
Gender: Masculine. Planet: Sun. Element: Fire. Chakras: Sacral, Base. Deities: Eos, Athena, Hermes. Magickal powers: This flowering herb is good for use in prosperity, for money drawing energies. A healing tool, it will bring sexual prowess to men and women. Medicinally: saffron is an all-around healing agent. Used for pain in many cultures, it has a slight sedative way about it, to calm nerves, and also to help cancer patients have an appetite. Any loss of appetite, saffron added will help digestion.

Recipe of the Day: "*Saffron Artichokes and Almonds*"
Ingredients:
1 cup dried figs
1 cup boiling water
¼ teaspoon saffron threads
½ cup olive oil
4 pounds baby artichokes, halved and chokes removed
1 teaspoon kosher salt, or to taste
½ cup Spanish Marcona almonds
¼ cup white wine
1 teaspoon paprika
Directions:
1. Place figs in a bowl and cover with the boiling water. Allow the figs to plump for 5 minutes, then remove. Sprinkle ¼ teaspoon of saffron threads into the remaining liquid, and allow to steep for 5 minutes.
2. Heat olive oil in a large skillet over medium-high heat. Add artichokes, and toss until coated with oil. Pour in saffron water and salt. Bring to a boil, then reduce heat to medium-low, cover, and simmer until the artichokes are tender, about 8 minutes.
3. Uncover the artichokes and increase heat to medium-high. Add the figs, almonds, vinegar, and paprika. Cook and stir until all of the liquid has evaporated. Remove from the heat, recover, and allow to stand for 5 minutes before serving. Prepping: 25, cook 15 minutes. We're eating in 40 minutes.

This lovely saffron (I love this word) recipe comes straight from Talking head.

DAY 25:
"A peacefulness follows any decision, even the wrong one."
~ Author: Rita Mae Brown

We people, we like to do something, anything even if it is the wrong thing. Just as long as we can make a decision of what next step to do, then we are more restful, at peace. We are unsure of our own choices, unable to believe that our heart may be telling us what spirit wants, but then we make a choice, going ahead, and we get some kind of relief at least for a while. This is why many different forms of religions, faith systems, have rituals. Rituals let us do something. We can pray, light a candle, hug a tree, but it gives us the choice to do something about our situations. It relieves man's inherent need to work, to strive, to achieve a goal. Making decisions, then following through isn't always easy. We find ourselves in the midst of chaos if we have made a wrong one. Yet there are always options. We may think we have no way out, no choices, are stuck, but we never are. Continue to meditate, continue to do our daily rituals, continue to make decisions, Spirit will help us.

Animal Totem of the Day: Hawk.
Hawk has been flying over my yard the last few days. Hawk brings messages from the gods. WE have a signal, a clue about the magick of life. This magick can give us power to overcome a stressful or difficult situation. Do we have powers that we are not using? Hawk's calls, cry, shriek is to pierce our unawareness, make us aware, and get the answers we need. Watch for the details of life, the littlest one, the sign, the omen; anything that tells us the answers when we watch Hawk.

Stone of the Day: Tiger Eye.
Tiger Eye is an 18th Anniversary gemstone. Gender: Male. Chakras: Sacral Chakra, Solar Plexus Chakra. Zodiac: Capricorn. Planet: Sun, Element: Fire, Earth. Deities: Ra, Sol, Athena, Venus, Aphrodite. The tiger's eye is an all-around healing stone. Known by the pharaohs, the wise men of Ancient Egypt to even now, the rich have tiger's eye around them. The eye of the Tiger shows power, wisdom, and knowledge in how to provide, to draw the necessary needs. Medicinally: Tiger's eye is well known to be carried for protection, for all around healing, the heart, the blood system, hormonal imbalance.

Herb of the Day: Vanilla.

Gender: Masculine. Planet: Jupiter. Element: Fire. Chakras: Sacral, base, 3rd eye, crown. Deities: Juno, Venus, Aries. Magickal powers: draws love, worn by the ancients as an aphrodisiac. Medicinally: Vanilla in many cultures has been thought to help different aspects of the immune systems. But modern western herbal tends to believe it only good for its relaxing healing help. There are schools of thought that vanilla has a slight sedative aspect but there is no factual research on this. We do know the aromatherapy scent is both relaxing and love Drawing. Venus' favorite herb.

Recipe of the Day: "*Vanilla Popcorn*"

Ingredients:

¼ cup corn oil

1 (4 inch) vanilla bean, split lengthwise - make sure we use vanilla bean, not the extract. This will make the corn soggy.

¾ cup unpopped popcorn

1 tablespoon superfine sugar

Salt to taste

2 tablespoons butter, melted

Directions:

Heat corn oil in a large pot over medium-high or high heat for a minute. Add one kernel of popcorn to the oil. When the kernel pops, pour in the remaining popcorn and the vanilla bean. Place a lid on the pot, and shake gently until the corn starts to pop. Shake vigorously until the popping subsides.

Remove from the heat, and pour into a large bowl. Remove the vanilla bean from the corn. Scrape seeds from the vanilla bean, and mix with sugar. Stir sugar, salt and melted butter into the corn until evenly coated, and serve.

*Karen Bush on **allsrecipe.com** is a great contributor to good popcorn.*

DAY 26:
"Fear is a darkroom where negatives develop." ~ Usman B. Asif

We get this picture in our head. It is not something we have seen, perhaps we have heard it, but we imagine this scene, we envision it in our head. We start out with this wild boar in the room. Next we have not only a pink wild boar but purple polka dots on it. This wild boar has become bigger, stronger, more fierce, more ready to attack, to create havoc, then even just a few minutes ago. We brought the negative of what we think to a dark place, where we develop not only the reality but into something much more fearful than the situation may actually really be. Fear is our worst enemy. It comes to us stealing our peace, our joy, even creating arguments; fights with people we love who have no clue why we are upset. Our best spiritual advice: face the fear, see it for what it really is, and then break it down sending it out in dust particles to the universe. As Roosevelt said, "There is nothing to fear, but fear itself" as fear will destroy us. There is always a way if there is a will, so as we develop our pictures, let fear go. Task for today: Face one fear, smile at it, knowing that tomorrow the changes will come.

Animal totem of the Day: Wild boar.
His totem is one of the most powerful and its gifts are many. Boar is the totem of prosperity and spiritual strength. It is also a strong protector totem. Boar is the master of its domain and can teach you that same self-reliance. With Boar's help, you can face all of life's problems head on and emerge the stronger for it. It is a fearless guide through any tribulations you may face on your life path. Since Boars root around in the dirt, this totem is very connected to Mother Earth and is an excellent grounding totem. Before grounding, imagine you are Boar, low to the earth, standing firm and strong, and digging deeply into Mother Earth.

Stone of the Day: Topaz.
Gender: Masculine. Chakras: Sacral Chakra, Solar Plexus Chakra. Zodiac: Leo, Scorpio, Sagittarius. Element: Air. Magickal Powers: Topaz is a soothing stone, stimulates energies to the parts of our auras, and bodies. This is a stone of truth. Drawing love, joy, and blessings into our homes, we see that topaz will take stress out of any situation. Medically we have been known to carry topaz to aid in our digestive

tracts, heal eating disorders i.e. anorexia, or bulimia. The topaz will help us have an appetite in the process balancing the metabolism to speed up so we don't gain weight. A win–win stone.

Herb of the Day: Lemon Balm.
Gender: Feminine. Planet: Moon. Element: Water. Chakras: Base, 3rd eye, Crown. Deities: Diana, Venus, Artemis.
Magickal powers: this herb draws love, fertility, romance. As good an aphrodisiac as oysters on the shell, we see love in this herb. Medically this herb is a good anti- depressant, an astringent, a good cleanser for extra oily skin. Vitamin C.

Recipe of the Day: *"Lemon Sherbet"*
Ingredients:
2 cups white sugar
2 cups water
6 leaves lemon balm
1 cup Muscat wine
2 tablespoons lemon juice
Directions:
Bring the sugar, water, and lemon balm to a simmer in a saucepan over medium heat. Stir until the sugar has dissolved. Strain into a heatproof container. Stir in the Muscat wine. Refrigerate until cold, about 4 hours.
Stir in the lemon juice; pour the chilled mixture into an ice cream maker and freeze according to manufacturer's directions until it reaches "soft-serve" consistency. Transfer ice cream to a one- or two-quart plastic container with a lid; cover surface with plastic wrap and seal. For best results, ice cream should ripen in the freezer for at least 2 hours or overnight. - A variation is to add 6 sprigs mint, chopped to the water, lemon balm, sugar as it is boiling. We can prep this in about 10 minutes. Cook time 10 minutes; more prep time is overnight. Chill and eat in our hot days.

All over the internet, recipes for sherbet, sherbet, ices are shown. We just compiled this from a variety.

DAY 27:
"There are two basic motivating forces: fear and love. When we are afraid, we pull back from life. When we are in love, we open to all that life has to offer with passion, excitement, and acceptance. We need to learn to love ourselves first, in all our glory and our imperfections. If we cannot love ourselves, we cannot fully open to our ability to love others or our potential to create. Evolution and all hopes for a better world rest in the fearlessness and open-hearted vision of people who embrace life." ~ John Lennon

The morning is bright. The weather people say the temps are going to get into the hundreds today here. Yet this beautiful Tennessee morning has a slight breeze. Setting the sprinklers out early, so the little Asian Lilies, the tall sunflowers, the ornamental peppers, the other young plants whose purpose is to serve us. Yes, these living beings are quite beautiful, yet we often forget that the purpose, is take the carbon monoxide out of the air, put out positive oxygen. The seedlings soak up moisture, water from our earth, and then help hydrate the world we live in. Amazing that this tiny aster, white symbolizing purity, pink symbolizing healing, is also healing our world as we humans do our best to pollute the earth. This is the same thing fear does to us. Fear is our worst enemy. We battle it, pretending to the outside world that all is great, until fear grips us so tightly, we burst like as if we put a Mentos into a bottle of coke. We start doing actions, some that are wise, some not well thought about going on pure emotion, pure hurt, pure fear. Since fear is not a good feeling, nothing that comes from it will be good. What we put out is what will come out. If we open ourselves to all life has to offer, much like our lovely blooms in the garden opens to the bright sunshine, we have the ability to create, the ability to have vision, to truly love.

Animal totem of the Day: Butterfly.
The parking garage at VA hospital is dark, dank, hot. Yet as I went out to the car to pick up dad at the door, one beautiful black and gold butterfly flitted in to light on my car. I just had to stop, admire the beauty of this small delicate animal. In the midst of sickness, fear, worry, spirit sent me this gift to just remind me that even in the middle of the chaos, the doubts, the glimmer of beauty, of positivity is here for us all. The butterfly reminds us that our physical bodies, the physical world doesn't

matter. What counts is what is in our soul. Life is to dance, remember to not be so serious about everything. Go ahead, do the next thing we want to do, but bring color, joy, look for the positive, look for the happiness in the moment. All life changes, much like butterfly changes from larva caterpillar, to cocoon, to beautiful butterfly, we can as well change from a dark worried troubled soul to allowing the beauty of this one tiny moment, that little small hope to come into our lives. Dance in the garden through life with butterfly my friends. Dance.

Stone of the Day: Tourmaline.
Gender: Feminine. Chakras: Base. Zodiac: Virgo, Libra. Planet: Venus. Element: Earth. Deities: Gia, Zeus, Tara. Magickal powers: Tourmaline helps in repelling negativity in magickal rites; seals the doors so negative or dark entities can't enter the circle. A healing stone for understanding, it diminishes fears, doubts, and bitterness. It draws money, prosperity into our lives, with money rituals and rites. Medically: tourmaline has been known in many cultures to help with left – right brain balancing, healing paranoia, fears as well as healing hand- eye coordination.

Herb of the Day: Onions.
Gender: Masculine. Planet: Mars. Element: Fire. Chakras: Base, Solar Plexus, 3rd eye. Deities: Mars, Mercury, Artemis, Diana the hunter. Magickal Powers: Onions are very protective. Place them in any circle, the dark sides of the universe, can't enter into the rites. As onions absorb smells, tastes of other foods, so it absorbs the negativity from any rituals. Good for healing diseases in a sick room. Medically, onions are a good source of Vitamin C, E. In most cultures used for colds, flu, other virus healings.

Recipe of the Day: "*Onion Jam*"
Ingredients:
1/4 cup vegetable oil
1/2 cup white sugar
4 cups onion, coarsely chopped
1/4 teaspoon salt
Ground black pepper to taste
1/2 cup red wine vinegar
Directions:
Heat vegetable oil in a heavy skillet over medium heat.

Stir sugar into vegetable oil with a wooden spoon, stirring constantly until mixture is a light caramel-color, about 10 minutes. Mixture will be very hot.
Stir onion, salt, and black pepper into sugar mixture. Onions will immediately start to caramelize. Stir frequently over medium heat until sugar has dissolved and onions are browned, about 15 minutes.
Pour red wine vinegar into onion mixture and simmer until mixture has a jam consistency, about 30 minutes. Let cool to serve. Prep this jam in 15 minutes; cook it 55 minutes. Serve over cream cheese spread on crackers. Good for you, as well as quite tasty if we like onions. (Remember to brush our teeth as well as repelling demons with our breath, we may repel other people as well. This may be one reason why onions keep us from getting sick as no one wants to get close to us!)

Of course, we found bacon/onion jam, all sorts of jams but this one from Wendymarie67 on ***allsrecipe.com*** *is one we decided to play with.*

DAY 28:
"Miracles come in moments. Be ready and willing." ~ Wayne Dyer

"Don't do something stupid, just because we are temporarily upset." ~ lifeandlovequotesandsayings

The wind is blowing slightly this morning. The dogs lift their noses toward the wind sniffing the skunk smell. Here is in the south, there are times when Bro Skunk runs out from the woods. Not sure of his way, he gets in the way of cars. Neither the drivers or Brother Skunk are happy about this situation. Skunk's natural instinct is to use his protection, his spray to put up walls, barriers so that danger doesn't come near. We, as people, thank the gods, don't have a nasty smell, but we certainly know how to throw up the protective walls, the barriers that don't allow anyone in. Even in trying to keep the negative energies, the troubles away, we also have our hearts, our minds, our spirits, our bodies closed to the good ones. We get upset too quickly, not looking at the entire situation. We don't see that although right this minute this is uncomfortable, certainly not what we had planned, tomorrow, next week, next month, this moment is exactly where it should be. We shut up our chakras, act impulsively, immediately much like Bro Skunk; so we close up chakras, situations that may be helpful later. We just don't see it. Bro Skunk, he doesn't look first either. He closes everything off, but his defenses which keeps everything out. We close off our own chakras. Even if we feel sad, feel anger, feel hurt, this just indicates that we are still open to learn, to hope to feel. If we are numb, uncaring, we have closed ourselves off. We need to think first, don't do something stupid, because of a temporary upset, be ready, and be willing for miracles to come out of what will come!

Animal totem of the Day: Skunk.
Yuck, letting Bob, Bets, Cherokee, out this am first thing, I smell Skunk. Cherokee and Bob both try to turn the doorknob with their paws if old Grammee here is slow. The dogs recoil back as well. Old man Bob turns back, wanting to come back in, but I'm not having that. It really isn't that bad, girls and boys. (It actually is pretty bad, poor Bob). The message is clear this day. Skunk reminds us to keep our self-esteem strong, our respect for ourselves on target. A powerful medicine, both mystically,

magickally, we should always expect respect, even demand it. Skunk totem tells us that we should appreciate, understand our own talents, gifts, use them so we don't lose them. Skunk is peaceful. His medicine teaches us to balance out our interaction with others, remembering there are times to withdraw, draw the circle, and be patient. Skunk reminds us there is a time for solitude, alone time, for reflection, for peace. Spirit often leads us to other paths, no matter where we want to be.

Stone of the Day: Turquoise.
Turquoise is an 11th Anniversary gemstone. Some references have shown that the stone vibrates to the number 1. Gender: Masculine. Chakras: Heart Chakra, Throat Chakra, Third Eye Chakra. Birthstone: December. Zodiac: Scorpio, Sagittarius, Aquarius, Pisces. Planet: Venus & Neptune. Element: Earth/ Air/ Fire. Deities: Ra, Sol, Zeus, Athena, Hecate, Arcadia, Diana, Isis. Magickal Powers: Used in purification rituals, best known as a healing stone, Diseases, wounds, protection from infection, even protection of pollutants in the air. Medically the holistic world uses this stone to help with mood swings, depression, protects the nervous system and the heart. The blood stream is healed through better absorption of nutrients, boosting the immune system.

Herb of the Day: Poppy.
Gender: Feminine. Planet: Moon. Element: Water. Chakras: Throat, Base, 3rd eye. Deities: Venus, Athena, Diana, Hermes. Magickal powers: Eating of the poppy seeds as long been used as a charm to help women get pregnant, also draws love. (If we need to take a drug test at work, don't eat for a few days before hand, you will test positive for opiates or hemp) Carrying poppy seeds for money drawing is part of the Old Craft. Medicinally: Poppy is well known to relieve pain. Remember though that opium, morphine, etc. are all derivatives of poppy. This can cause hallucinations.

Recipe of the Day: *"Cranberry – Poppy Mayonnaise"*
Ingredients:
1/2 cup mayonnaise - to make the best mayonnaise use the basic recipe to make homemade mayo. If we are allergic to eggs or a vegan find an eggless mayo recipe ****
1/2 cup whole berry cranberry sauce
1 teaspoon poppy seeds

Directions:
Whisk together mayonnaise and cranberry sauce in a large bowl. Stir in the poppy seeds. Refrigerate until serving. Prep time is 5 minutes
Homemade mayonnaise:
To make 1 cup of mayonnaise you will need:
1 cup of light olive oil (less strongly flavored than standard olive oil) or other good-quality oil, like walnut or sweet almond oil
1 egg
Juice of 1 lemon, or vinegar
A pinch of salt (and pepper, if desired)
Water to thin the mayonnaise
2. Separate the egg. Reserve the whites for other recipes.
3. Egg yolks contain a natural emulsifier, lecithin, which helps thicken sauces and bind ingredients.
4. Lemon juice or vinegar adds acidity and flavor to the mayonnaise.
For each cup of mayonnaise, add between 1 and 2 tablespoons of fresh lemon juice or vinegar, depending upon your tastes.
5. Combine the egg and acid in the bowl, whisking to mix.
You can make mayonnaise in a food processor or by hand, with a mixing bowl and whisk. The key for either method is to add oil very slowly, in a steady stream, while the processor is running or you're whisking vigorously. (Note: to stabilize a lightweight mixing bowl, set it on a coiled kitchen towel.)
6. Continue to whisk constantly, adding the oil in a slow, steady stream.
If the mayonnaise starts looking too thick, add enough water to thin it to the consistency you desire. Add about a teaspoon of water at a time.
When the oil is all mixed in, the mayonnaise should be thick and fluffy, with your whisk forming ribbons through the mixture.
If it never thickened and you're stirring a puddle, chances are you will need to start over. (Or, if you're still partway through the process, you can save the emulsion by adding another egg yolk, whisking vigorously. Add in remaining oil, plus extra for a double recipe), and adjust the seasonings.

Allsrecipe.com contributor just "tahoegirl" shared this one. We loved it, added to it.

DAY 29:

"Everybody needs beauty as well as bread, places to play in and pray in, where nature may heal and give strength to body and soul." ~ John Muir

The clouds, puffy white, nestled on top of the majestic mountains. Driving through these tall wonders, the beauty of it all just took my breath away. Although coming out here to meet everyone, suddenly I knew I needed this moment in time. Just as I reached the point that mountain side touched mountain, trees stood straight, tall, brilliance of color bursting out in bright sunlight, Lynyrd Skynyrd's Free Bird came on the radio. Oh, to soar to the highest heights of the mountains, to sit among the gods, pondering life. Life May not be so easy. Things may go wrong on the trip, the airline, the car, or the turnout not so great at the meet and greet but the ones who are supposed to be there will be. I can recover things lost by the airline. At the moment, the top of the mountains smiling down on me, I find my beauty, find my rest, find the peace, the hope I am looking for.

Animal totem of the Day: Condor.

Another messenger of the gods, this totem brings life, death, rebirth, and the prayers to the gods. Communing in the clouds with spirit, this huge bird soars high above life's problems to he answers. The medicine of condor alerts us that we are protected by spirit always. There is a sacred Inca prophecy about the Eagle and the Condor. It addresses how the mental and materialistic energy of the Eagle (which represents North America) has dominated the spiritual and compassionate energy of the Condor (which represents South America). The prophecy speaks of a time when the Eagle of the North and the Condor of the South will fly together and the Earth will come into balance.

Stone of the Day: Unakite.

Gender: Feminine. Chakras: Heart Chakra. Zodiac: Scorpio. Planet: Mars & Venus. Element: Fire & Water. Deities: Mars, Mercury, Venus, Athena, Isis. Magickal powers: This stone is for rituals of vision, and healing. Unakite is in grounding and centering rites. Medically: the stone is supporting of recovering healing from major illness. We can heal reproductive system, with giving pregnancies a helping hand. Be cautious though, as Unakite enhances weight gain.

Herb of the Day: Thyme.
Gender: Feminine. Planet: Venus. Element: Water. Chakras: Solar Plexus, Crown. Magickal Powers: rites of sleep, dream healing, we use this herb for cleansing, protection of repelling negativity. Medically: the Old craft ways uses thyme as an anti-bacterial, an antibiotic, and antiseptic. When we have puffiness, swelling of feet, hands, eating thyme in our foods is a great diuretic. There are some methods of using thyme for lowering high temperatures. We can make a great bug/insect repellant by using both the leaves and the flowers.

Recipe of the Day: "*Cheddar/Thyme Biscuits*"
Ingredients:
2 cups flour
4 teaspoons baking powder
3 tablespoons white sugar
½ teaspoon salt
½ teaspoon cream of tartar
½ cup butter or margarine
¾ cup milk
½ cup shredded Cheddar cheese
1 tablespoon chopped fresh thyme
Directions:
Preheat the oven to 425 degrees F (220 degrees C).
In a medium bowl, stir together the flour, baking powder, sugar, salt and cream of tartar. Cut in butter using a pastry cutter or a fork until it is the size of peas. Make a well in the center of the mixture and measure the milk, cheese and thyme into the bowl. Gently mix until a soft dough forms.
Roll or pat out on a floured surface to ¾ inch thick. Cut into circles and place on a baking sheet.
Bake for 10 minutes in the preheated oven, or until the bottoms of the biscuits are golden brown. Prepping time is only 10 minutes. We can cook this in 10 minutes, so in 25 minutes we are ready to share these lovely biscuits. Great with fish or chicken.

Laura902's recipe on ***allsrecipe.com*** *sprang out to us, but there were several others as well.*

DAY 30:

"In my room, the world is beyond my understanding, but when I walk I see that it consists of three or four hills and a cloud." ~Wallace Stevens

The five year old mind looks at the most mundane items, such as a stick, a rock that he/she has picked up off the ground. At once, this object becomes a magick wand, or a token to be given to the fairies to take them to the clouds to play. Or perhaps, he sees a writing tool, so he can draw in the sand, the wondrous pictures he has thought of to share with family, friends, or just the fairies that dance around him. The stone gets added to others soon to build an ant house, or a wall to capture the fairies. This youth this innocence has a bigger mind, a more open mind to see possibilities when we have allowed fear, worry, to creep in to take over the brilliant ideas, the wonderful dreams that spirit has given us. This quote may not make sense to some, but it reminds us that what we perceive when we look at things is what we see, what is our reality. Sometimes the answer is much more simple; the way of the path is easier than we have in our minds. The laws of nature, the laws of attraction, the laws of love, are the same. What we send out to the universe, what we see, is what we will get back. Today the sun is shining; the Tennessee morning is alive with sound, with a quiet gentle breeze that will help dry the sheets hanging in the wind, with that fresh air smell we don't get in the dryer! We can see that the garden is growing tall. The wheat germ in the front bed is ready to give new seeds, be picked, the bush beans have buds. Morning glories have lifted their heads, opening up to the sun with a beauty along the rail to the deck. Everywhere I look we can see something wonderful, a miracle, as to show us that there is something more that has our lives in hand. We can see great news, more love, and happiness everywhere we look. Our world is at the beginning of a fresh new day, ready for greatness, ready for miracles to come.

Animal totem of the Day: Grasshopper.

The tiniest little grasshopper got in the house. Before my 3 wild ones could pounce on him, I managed to capture him in a cup, to take him back out to the green grass. See, grasshopper never jumps backwards; Sister Hopper only keeps jumping ahead. She sees possibilities -truthfully her medicine is don't think too much!! Jump in, move forward with positive belief we are jumping into the right places.

Stone of the Day: Blue Lace Agate.
Gender: Feminine. Chakras: Throat Chakra. Zodiac: Pisces. Planet: Neptune. Element: Water, Air. Deities: Neptune, Ariel, Poseidon, Ogden, Athena, Uriel. Magickal powers: This stone looks cool, peaceful, and she draws peace to us. She is a healer of communication, allowing magickal rituals to flow easily with the use of Blue Lace to be able to express the chants, the needs. This blue lace agate repels anger, bitterness, and heartache. Medically the old ways say this stone will help strengthen the bones, the joints. Helping with healing eyes, and irritants, carrying this stone helps with eyesight.

Herb of the Day: Walnut.
Gender: Masculine. Planet: Sun. Element: Fire. Chakras: Base, Heart, Throat. Deities: Hermes, Ra, Aphrodite. Magickal powers: We use this in rituals of fertility, sexuality, love, passion. Medically, this nut is usually full of protein, will give nutrients to the blood stream, and help with the heart building tools.

Recipe of the Day: "*Raspberry Walnut Baked Brie*"
Ingredients:
1 sheet frozen puff pastry, thawed
1 (8 ounce) round Brie cheese
1/3 cup seedless raspberry jam
2 tablespoons chopped walnuts
Directions:
Preheat oven to 350 degrees F (175 degrees C). Line a baking sheet with aluminum foil and lightly grease with cooking spray. Lay the puff pastry onto the prepared baking sheet. Center the Brie wheel onto the pastry. Spread the jam evenly over the top of the Brie. Sprinkle the walnuts atop the jam. Fold the puff pastry over the top of the Brie, sealing all openings. Bake in preheated oven until the pastry is golden brown, about 20 minutes. Prep time is 10 minutes, cooking time 20 minutes; we are serving appetizers to our friend in 30 minutes!

We found the best one on allsrecipe.com came from LauraKKH, but we found many more.

Day 31:
"I'm happy to report that my inner child is still ageless."
~ James Broughton

"The child is in me still and sometimes not so still." ~ Fred Rogers, The World According to Mister Rogers: Important Things to Remember

"Everyone is born creative; everyone is given a box of crayons in kindergarten. Then when you hit puberty they take the crayons away and replace them with dry, uninspiring books on algebra, history, etc. Being suddenly hit years later with the 'creative bug' is just a wee voice telling you, 'I'd like my crayons back, please." ~ Hugh MacLeod

"I don't wanna grow up, I'm a Toys"R"Us kid." ~ commercial from Toys"R"Us

This am I already had started a blog on trust, but then the weight of the morning news, the dreary day where the prediction of yet another bout of cold weather is going to creep in, said Agh! When did I get 60 AND when did I grow up? We all have these days when responsibilities, being "mature" being "adult", just seems to get on our nerves. To think that we have to ALWAYS be the strong one, the serious one, the one stepping up, taking action can not only be quite daunting, but also annoying. See, when we are the only ones taking charge, taking actions, we are the only ones who can be blamed when something goes wrong. People watching in hindsight, can easily tell us what we should have, could have done, yet when we offer to step back, allow someone else to pave the way through unchartered territories, we often find ourselves alone. Even in our love relationships, that special he/she that is Mr. or Ms. Right! We feel we are the only one! The great news is although to the naked eye, to the outside world, even to our logical, sensible adult mind we are alone, we are not!! We can go back to our inner child, find our first faith, that innocence, that belief system that comes with imagination to imagine that we can achieve the impossible! We have the strength, we have the power, we have the gift of our minds, as long as the spiritual world, the universe around us so we know we are never alone, we can be the child putting his/her hand in the Great Spirit's, walking the path with truth, with faith, with hope.

(deborahmillspsychic, Daily Doses of Deborah, Vol III Lessons on Hope, 2014)

Animal totem of the Day: Ant.

Bro Ant is the worker of the world. Carrying weights 10 times more than he actually weighs, his medicine teaches us that yes we can carry the weight of the world on our shoulders; we just have to get some help from the gods upstairs. Only great imagination, only great belief can help Bro Ant take care of his needs, his family, in his consistent, persistent relentless ability to never give up. This totem reminds us we may feel small and alone, but we are mighty in our belief, our strengths.

"There are so many wonderful stones, recipes; Moonzies Healing Stones and Grammee's Goodies to Go have lots of info, ideas, thoughts all compiled by many contributors. We thank each and every one."

There were many different references that I used in making this book. Most of the writings are mine with the quotes referenced to the right people. The recipes are compiled from a couple of difference sources on the internet, but most have some variation of my own. Stones, both metaphysical and magickal references, along with the herbs were also compiled from several different sites, but combined in my words. I am referencing the sites I used at the end of the writing.
The whole of the universe is set up for our use, our purpose, to provide our needs, our lives, our wants, our desires, our dreams. Whether we use the Old Craft to magickally bring or draw our hopes to manifest or we use these tools in logical, earth plane ways, all of nature, all of the universe, all of our spiritual world is at our fingertips. Our dreams are only minutes away.

References:
Wikipedia.com
Linsdomain.com
Animal totems.com
Charms of light.com
Martha Stewart.com
Allsrecipes.com
Best Crystals.com
Wicca 101.com

May the fairies dance around each of us today. May the universe bless us as we continue to learn, continue to grow. Love ya

www.ingramcontent.com/pod-product-compliance
Ingram Content Group UK Ltd.
Pitfield, Milton Keynes, MK11 3LW, UK
UKHW041923190726
13854UKWH00003B/1405

9 781304 935199